THIS TOO IS DIPLOMACY

*To Midge Carney + Loretta Mahoney
With warmest regards,
Dorothy J. Irving*

October, 2008

THIS TOO IS DIPLOMACY

Stories of a Partnership

by

Dorothy J. Irving

Bloomington, IN  Milton Keynes, UK

AuthorHouse™
1663 Liberty Drive, Suite 200
Bloomington, IN 47403
www.authorhouse.com
Phone: 1-800-839-8640

AuthorHouse™ *UK Ltd.*
500 Avebury Boulevard
Central Milton Keynes, MK9 2BE
www.authorhouse.co.uk
Phone: 08001974150

© *2007 Dorothy J. Irving. All rights reserved.*

No part of this book may be reproduced, stored in a retrieval system, or transmitted by any means without the written permission of the author.

First published by AuthorHouse   7/30/2007

ISBN: 978-1-4343-0250-2 (sc)

Library of Congress Control Number: 2007901953

Printed in the United States of America
Bloomington, Indiana

This book is printed on acid-free paper.

For Fred
Who led us on the journey

For Sue, Rick, Barbara
Who traveled much of the way with us

For Erik, Emilie, Tulsi, Alex,
Hira, Chandi, Asha, Jaya,
The next generation,
Who are waiting to read it

When I was a child, as my mother brushed my curls, she often said, "Dorothy, your hair parts in a double crown. That means you'll live under a different flag some day."

In 1952 my husband and I attended a large meeting in an auditorium filled with Foreign Service Officers. I looked around that Washington room, and with a deep sense of pride and belonging, thought, "Any person in this room would go anywhere in the world tomorrow morning if asked."

So would I.

CONTENTS

Foreword xiii

BEFORE

First Decision 1
Career Choice 6
Cast Of Characters 8

THE FOREIGN SERVICE YEARS

Vienna 1952-54
First Trip 13
Occupied City 17
Broken Leg 24
Himmelstrasse 28

New Zealand 1960-62
Stopover in Fiji 35
I Meet The Press 39
Mr. Thwaites 43
Fire! 46
Oyster Crackers? 50

Along The Way
Foreign Service Children 55
Surgeries Abroad 59
Calm at Five 64

Return To Vienna 1967-68
- Life at Linneplatz 69
- Rank Has its Privileges—Junior Style 74
- Those Who Drove 78

Along The Way
- Heart Attack 85
- Ambassador? 89
- Rebecca 94

Iceland 1972-76
- The Challenge 99
- Arrival in Iceland 101
- Home(s) 105
- Do you speak …? 108
- Learning from the Top-Names in Iceland 112
- Cold War Incident 115
- Northern Winter 118
- Winter Sports 121
- "No, Mrs. Irving, No Brownies!" 124
- Little People 127
- Pipes and Pumps 129
- Hamrahlid Choir 135
- Houseguests 137
- To Suit The Occasion 140
- Foreign Service Pets 144
- Roundup 148
- City Hospital 151
- Diplomatic Cable 155
- Diplomatic Language 157

President Nixon's Visit 161
Moment of Pride 167
Sendiherrafrúin 170

Along The Way
Bara Tia Dropa 175
I Won't Go In 178
There Are No Ants In Iceland 181
D. C. Day Care 182

Jamaica 1977-79
Assignment: Jamaica 187
Security In A Tense Land 191
Bonnie 196
A Cup Of Tea 201
The Button Basket 203
Flowers I Have Known 207
The Woman at Red Hills 211
Teacher Abroad 213

We Come Home
Most Recent Occupation 221
Happy Fourth Of July (First Year At Home) 223
These Shoes Walked At Ephesus 227
Retirement 230
Stairs Of My Life 233

Acknowledgments 237
About the Author 239

Foreword

Who, better than I, to write the foreword, for I was the first in line to benefit from Dorothy's activities. She often set the tone and atmosphere that contributed to the many successes our embassy achieved, to the many successes that were officially attributed to me. This series of stories—all true—describe some of the ways she reached out that made a difference in our relations with each host country.

Nations are made up of people. The more we understand the culture and perspective of others—even when we disagree—the greater our chances of building bridges and changing opinions. The purpose of diplomacy is to advance a nation's interests in the world without resorting to war. In this book, Dorothy Irving shows us that diplomacy is more than formal protocol. In addition to relating some of her activities that played an important substantive role, there are many stories that describe her role as the wife of an American ambassador and an American mother abroad. Her activities came to the favorable attention of the overseas public. Wherever she lived she made friends for the United States.

Because she was so effective, and even though the Department of State does not "officially" recognize the substantive contribution a spouse can make, Dorothy was one of a very limited number of spouses (she may have been the first) to be granted a full-field security clearance. One can legitimately call her the "unpaid equal."

Dorothy Irving's activities abroad, directly and indirectly, demonstrate that *This Too Is Diplomacy*.

Frederick Irving
(U.S. Ambassador, retired)

BEFORE

On our first date we decided to get married.
On our second we chose our career.

We never regretted either decision.

First Decision

"When did you know you were going to marry Grandpa?" A teenage grandchild once asked me. "Was there a special minute? Do you remember?"

Indeed, I remember—the place, the moment, the time of day. The place was the old Biltmore Hotel in Providence, Rhode Island, in its 1945 version before the modern makeover. The Biltmore was appropriate. It had been host to high school proms we had both attended—though not together; its ballroom had long been a respected center of Providence social life. The hotel even had a large lobby clock to "meet under" during those wartime years. The month was June of 1945, near the end of World War II, after V-E Day and before V-J Day. Fred had just returned from three months overseas in the Air Force, flying in combat out of Italy, and from nine more months in a Prisoner of War camp in Germany after his plane was shot down the previous August. I was visiting Providence for a few days, and a high school classmate had arranged that the three of us would meet at the Biltmore after Fred attended a family graduation earlier in the evening. As we two waited, we both knew we were very eager to see Fred again. We didn't know lightning would strike.

It had been arranged to meet at the hotel's cocktail lounge on the second floor. Wide stairs curved up from the main lobby, leading to the lounge on the right and a large dining room on the left—two rooms that merged into one large open area. From our carefully chosen seat on a banquette in the lounge, classmate Bill and I could see the stairs and anyone ascending them. After some time, Fred appeared, wearing his tan Air Force summer uniform with cap tucked into the belt, in the Air Force custom. He turned to the left and entered the dining room; I stood up in excitement. He looked around the dining area; I sat down, thinking, "Girls don't stand up when they see boys, the boys come to them." Still not seeing us, he turned to come towards the lounge; I stood up again. Again I sat down. I managed this jack-in-the-box bit four times before he reached us. Fred, of course, hadn't seen it, and I cannot begin to imagine what Bill thought, but that was the moment: 10:30 PM on a June evening in 1945, when Fred Irving walked up those stairs at the Providence Biltmore Hotel.

We had first met as sophomores in high school—almost nine years earlier—when we were both assigned to homeroom 8-R. There were twenty-six of us in 8-R that year, four rows of five each and the row by the wall with six. Mrs. Grant had her teacher's desk in the center front. Both kind and strict, she made sure we toed the mark. Fred says he knew from that first shared year that I was "the girl," but that I was slow to see it. He also says he couldn't ask me out because he had no money to take me anywhere. I say he could have suggested a walk. But these conversations come from much later and not from that time in school. I do remember that in Room 8-R there was a very thin boy named Fred Irving with beautiful dark eyes and kindness that showed through even at fifteen. I do not remember anyone else in the room.

In Junior and Senior years we again shared homerooms. In Junior year we had Miss Sherman, who sat, in her almost-floor-length dresses, behind a large wooden desk on a raised platform at the front of the room. She wore her hair in a bun and appeared to squint through her glasses. It seemed she saw nothing, but she knew everything that went on in Room 6 and always knew when the students in our back right corner were talking or passing notes. Besides ruling our homeroom, she taught us Latin and English. Our Senior year Mistress of Ceremonies (no other phrase would fit stylish, black-haired Miss Day) was also a teacher of Latin and English. In her room the boys sat in the rows near the door, the girls in rows near the windows. Warm friendships come to mind as I picture that room: Kathy, Alice, Abigail, Dorothy; Elmer, Dante, George, Fred.

In addition to shared homerooms, your grandfather and I met in several classes: English with the young and dashing Mr. Kenworthy—he of the green over-the-shoulder book bag, who liked to read us literature he loved, and who sat on the chair back to do it; motherly, trustworthy Mrs. Piche, who taught us German and directed my many efforts in the Dramatic Club. (At one play where I had the lead, Fred remembers ushering my parents to their seats.) When we visited Mrs. Piche after our marriage, she told us she had always known I was helping Fred with his translations (sometimes right in class), and she had often thought that more than fluent German might develop from this collaboration. The two of us were also in honors classes together, and as Seniors we ran for class office. Neither of us won. In all these activities there were many friends who did things together. Because he worked forty hours a week in addition to studying the minimum three-hours per night our homework demanded, Fred participated less than some. But Classical was a high school where everyone was friendly and mixed casually. I enjoyed the friendships and fun, but was far from serious about any boys I went out with. At fifteen, I wasn't giving a thought to marriage or commitment. College and "career" lay ahead.

In 1939 we graduated and went off to college, Fred to Brown, and I to Mount Holyoke. That same year my family moved out of town. My only link with high school friends became my visit to Providence each summer and an occasional card or letter.

When Fred went into the Air Force, he and I began to correspond regularly. When he went overseas, we wrote every week. I told myself it was my patriotic duty to write to "our boys in service." I did not think it odd that my "patriotism" extended to only one person.

Throughout his months in Italy and throughout his POW months, letters were sent off faithfully. When I visited my parents, they used to enjoy hearing parts of Fred's letters from the war and from prison camp. In World War II, ships were the main means of transport. To save precious shipboard space, letters had to be written on stationery called "V-Mail," small pieces of paper that formed their own envelopes. We were all urged to be careful about what we wrote in those V-Mails. Letters might be read by Army censors, or (during the POW days) by prison camp guards. Posters on the home front, read, "Loose Lips Sink Ships" or "Think before you Write or Speak." They warned that any seemingly unimportant fact could be pieced together with other small facts and give the enemy vital information. So I wrote carefully of small daily doings, often about the third grade class I was teaching. I wondered if third grade antics would seem very exciting to men risking their lives, but your grandfather later said the stories brought a welcome touch of home. After the war we learned that not all the V-Mails had reached the prisoners. When the Allied forces liberated the camps, they found stacks of undistributed mail and packages.

When word came in 1945 that Fred was found and released, I was teaching in Somerville, New Jersey, where I boarded at Mrs. Smith's home on Middaugh Street with three other female teachers. Mrs. Smith, a widow, had moved her own bedroom to the dining room and rented out each of her four immaculate bedrooms upstairs. She worked as a truant officer for the Somerville schools, and the schools helped her find teacher tenants. The four of us that year became good friends. We often ate out together in the evenings, and we attended USO dances together. We suffered together for Beatrice, whose husband was missing in the Battle of the Bulge that long winter of 1944 and who never was to come home. Mathilda, the cheeriest member of our group, and a woman who always knew she wanted to get married and raise a family, kept a card file of all the men we met or corresponded with. She kept mine until the May evening the phone call came. It was long distance from Providence, from the boy I would be waiting with that June night at the Biltmore.

"Dorothy," Bill said, "We've just heard that Fred is safe and whole and coming home. I wanted to tell you right away."

Safe. Safe rang through my head, but even then I was slow to recognize how much this meant to me. I turned to my house mates clustered behind me at the phone and said, "Fred, the boy I've been writing to in Prison Camp, is coming home. I'm so glad."

I thought that was it. But Mathilda, more astute than I in affairs of the heart, went right upstairs from that front hall, got out the Dorothy Petrie file box and tore up all my cards but one. I still didn't sense that my life had changed, but I felt a growing excitement about seeing him in person once again.

Finally, at the Biltmore, when he appeared at the top of those stairs, I did know that this was the man with whom I wanted to spend my life. And, once I knew, I was never shaken. Shortly after Fred arrived that June night, Bill left us for his evening job at the local radio station. Fred and I walked the streets of Providence, talking and talking. We found ourselves in front of the old high school, where, at fifteen, I had been so unready to think seriously about a man in my life; now, at twenty-three, I was ready. We embraced before those tall iron gates.

"There is a wall between us," he said sadly. Did he mean a wall of no job? of different religions? of different economic levels? None of that mattered.

"Well," I said, "I certainly can't feel a wall."

Our first decision was made.

Career Choice

The marriage decision had been made standing in front of our old high school. The following night, as we walked the campus of Brown University, we chose our career. On that second date, we talked of our hopes for the future. I described applying to teach at a school in Turkey. "I feel the need to know other countries," I said.

"After seeing what war does to countries and to people," Fred answered, "I know there has to be a better way to solve problems between nations. I'd like to join the Foreign Service. If countries could talk out their disagreements, it would be better than shooting them out. I'd like to help build international understanding."

He paused, "How would you feel about such a life? It would mean living in many different places, not always wonderful ones, and moving between countries every few years. If you don't want to do it, I'll find another career."

I was moved at his dedication and pleased at how well our ideals compared. "We seem to match very well. I'd be proud to belong to the Foreign Service."

And so our career started. Fred went to Fletcher School of Law and Diplomacy that fall, and the following spring we were married and moved to Washington. Tours of duty in Washington and overseas followed for almost thirty years.

We always felt it was a joint career. In the 1950s, Fred would be the one earning the salary, but I would be, as he said, "The Unpaid Equal." We had made the decision together and we each felt we had responsibility for building bridges between countries.

The anecdotes that follow give a few glimpses of our life in those diplomatic years. They tell a little of what life was like for this Foreign Service family. Of our three children, we had two with us at our first post, three at the second, then two, then one and at our last post, none. In Austria they attended the American School of Vienna; in New Zealand, local schools; and, in Iceland, the high school at the NATO Base. We are grateful that they could remain with us until time to return home for college and grateful to have so many memories we share with them. It is to share some of those memories with others that I now write.

Cast Of Characters

First and foremost ("Fyrst og fremst" as they say in Iceland) is Fred, my husband. It was his assignments as a Career Foreign Service Officer that took our family on this journey. And it was his support and respect that enabled me to participate fully in embassy responsibilities and to play a substantive role in the work we hoped to accomplish. He may not appear in every piece, but he was always there.

Next comes our oldest child, Susan. In 1952 she crosses with us on the SS United States and enters Vienna as a child of three. She starts high school in New Zealand, finishes in the States and briefly returns to Vienna at eighteen. She comes to Iceland and Jamaica only on vacations.

Rick enters as Dickie, the ten-month old baby creeping his way across the Atlantic. He attends and hates school in New Zealand, is a homesick teenager when we return to Austria, and, like Sue, visits Iceland and Jamaica on vacations. For him, vacations include an Icelandic summer working with Barbara in a fish freezing plant. Along the way he grows up and becomes Rick.

Barbara makes her debut in Fiji, buying a blue plastic purse. Her first Vienna tour is in 1967. She is the only child still at home during our busy Icelandic years. Like us, she loved the country and learned the language. Then, she too went home to the States to college.

Finally is the writer: "I is I," as Jamaica's Rastafarians would put it. I am the wife, mother, diplomat, teacher, author. Since this is my book I appear in every story.

Before

You will also meet household helpers, drivers, diplomats; presidents and prime ministers; a pool attendant, a caterer, a librarian, a fire chief; teachers, doctors, waiters. We remember them all.

The sections are arranged chronologically and grouped by country. The sections titled "Along the Way" contain pieces that tell of our Stateside life between overseas assignments, or, as in "Foreign Service Children" and "Surgeries Abroad," may group the experiences from several posts.

As you wander through the essays, we send you the Jamaican wish, "Walk Good."

THE FOREIGN SERVICE YEARS
VIENNA 1952-54

The Journey Begins

First Trip

Vienna! "The Irvings have been assigned to Vienna. They'll sail in September on the SS-United States!"

Over phone and back yard fence the news spread down our street and through our northern Virginia neighborhood. How glamorous it all sounded: baskets of fruit and champagne in the stateroom; paper streamers thrown from ship to shore on departure; on arrival, operas, pastries, and palaces.

Our neighbors held a farewell party for this first diplomatic family going overseas. The host urged on us his family's steamer trunk—one of those wonderful standing trunks from the days of the great voyages.

"I'll bring it over," he said and arrived the next morning, the trunk balanced across his son's red wagon. Parents in our baby-sitting club offered free sitting for our ten-month-old son and three-year-old daughter. "You'll have a lot to do," they said.

We did have a lot to do. Medical exams, dental checkups, passport pictures. "Usually people put the baby on the mother's passport, Mrs. Irving." "No, I want him to have his own. Then he can travel with anyone." Dickie's first passport photo shows my shoulder and the collar of my dress as I held him, but the passport is in his name, and the only face is his, a ten-month-old baby with his own Diplomatic Passport!

We gathered information about our new post. The State Department Post Report described climate, customs, kinds of activities, and clothes. "Bring at least two years supply of shoes," it read. "Most Austrian feet are broader than American. Cobblers make shoes to order, but then they don't believe their own measurements. They always make the shoes 'just a little wider' to be sure." At Hecht's Department store I bought pumps in black, brown and blue, walked in them for a day at home to test them, then returned and bought duplicates. For Susan

I bought shoes for now and the next size up; I asked at her children's shoe store what drawings I should send for later sizes. We shopped for clothing for us all, gathered medicine that might or might not be available in occupied Vienna, wrote to friends of our upcoming departure, interviewed families who might rent our house, and went up to Massachusetts to say goodbye to my father. (My mother had died three years earlier.)

My father was thrilled because we would be making the trip to Europe he never made, and because the State Department was sending his daughter and her family first class. But he was also worried. He had read stories about spying and intrigue in Austria during this post-war period, about missing persons who were never accounted for. When he stood in his driveway to wave goodbye, I felt he did not expect to see us again.

After the Massachusetts trip, it was time to pack. and to value our possessions in a new way: by their weight. "Will it fit in our weight allowance?" became the daily judgment. The government had a strict limit on poundage. A limited number of pounds could be sent by surface transport, which would take several weeks and would arrive long after we did. One hundred pounds a person could go by airfreight, and should be awaiting us in Vienna. In addition two suitcases each and that steamer trunk would go with us as accompanied baggage.

We piled everything we hoped to take on the ping-pong table in the basement and put the bathroom scale on the floor next to it. Next to the ping-pong table we put the trunk and a card table to hold things we would carry in our suitcases. Every evening for two weeks we separated and weighed each item under consideration. Choosing for an indefinite stay in an unknown house in an unfamiliar city made decisions challenging. Books were especially difficult. "This book weighs two pounds, this one three. Which can I live without for a few years?" "Is four pounds for this picture too much? It's always been in our living room." "How about Dickie's push toy? It will help him learn to walk, and it's very light."

Finally the ping-pong table held three separate piles: one, things to go in the surface shipment; one, items to be put in storage during our absence (the unchosen books); and the third, things to be sent by air. That third group had clothing for the four of us, toys for our two children. Susan's metal dollhouse had been an easy choice for air; it was light weight, collapsible and played with constantly. Although heavier, her newly mastered tricycle went there, too. Some of Dickie's trucks made it. During our many weeks in a Vienna hotel we were glad for the choices we had made. The dollhouse was the first thing unpacked on arrival and much played with as it sat on the desk in their hotel room. The trucks drove around on the patterned carpet, and the trike rode from the children's room to ours and back.

When all was separated and packed, and the house rented, we left for New York the day before our sailing. Older, wiser Foreign Service wives had told me, "The first trip is the easy one. Later, when the children are older, it will be more difficult. You'll see." Very proud of my clever accomplishment of getting myself, my husband, and these two young children packed and on board our first ocean liner, I knew (then) that such wives were mistaken. "What could be harder than this!"

The next morning we took a taxi to the appointed pier on the Hudson, boarded the ship and looked for our stateroom.

It is true the Department of State sends its diplomats first class, but neither my father nor we realized it is always the cheapest first class. Also, any child under the age of six years was considered as a half person for space requirements. Our family of four had a small inside stateroom. It held two built-in single beds, now crowded by a crib squeezed between them. There was no indication of where the fourth person would sleep. When the wonderful steamer trunk was opened, it looked like an upright side by side refrigerator-freezer: it filled the four square feet of free space. Drawers for sweaters, underwear, shoes lined its left half; the right had built in hangers for our week's on-board clothing optimistically including a long gown! Very plush, but there was no place to stand while unpacking. To look in the mirror we had to push the trunk's two sides shut. To reach the bath we had to crawl across one of the beds, inch around the slightly shorter crib, and cross the second bed. My husband and I looked at each other. "It's going to be a long four days."

But two things saved the trip. First, a friendly cabin steward told us the cabin next to ours was vacant. "It's only a single, but it might help," he offered. Indeed it did. We slept across the Atlantic in the two rooms—one child and one parent in each. We were even able to unpack enough to dress for the black tie dinner the last night on board. The same helpful steward had alerted us that there were no baby-sitting arrangements on the ship. "Sometimes," he said, "the playroom nurse will sit after her daytime duties." My husband hurried immediately to the playroom and hired her for the three evenings. After we fed the children at the early dinner, we left them with their sitter in the small cabin. She read and played games until both children fell asleep. When we returned from dinner we moved the baby to the crib. The first evening I came down mid-dinner to see if everything was all right. It was, and when I saw two very young children climbing on the water fountain and playing unsupervised tag in the hallway, the exorbitant sitting fee seemed worth it.

Our family used the hall not for tag, but for creeping. Dickie, at ten months, had just mastered this method of moving and needed to do it every day. Each morning, as other passengers went to the pet deck to walk their dogs and cats, I walked at Dickie's side as he moved up and down the first class corridors on his hands and knees, progressing at his own speed. And each morning we lifted a few more baby food jars, his meals for the day, out of his father's briefcase. This had seemed the safest way to carry his food for the journey—accessible and without breakage. We didn't realize how much we were in tune with our destination: most Viennese briefcases, whether carried by laborers or bank presidents, revealed lunch inside.

The four days went more quickly than expected. With young children and small quarters, we never quite felt the glamour of the voyage, but we did feel excitement as we approached this first overseas post. Would we find the operas, pastries, and palaces our neighbors had anticipated? We disembarked at Le Havre, took the boat train to Paris, and flew to Vienna. What lay ahead for us and our children was unknown.

Occupied City

Vienna, 1952. Vienna, drab and gray; gray with dust, with rain, with holes where ornate buildings once stood; gray where the bombed out opera house had once held the heart of the city; its people gray with years of war, with years of worry, dressed in clothing worn for too long a time.

Vienna, city of music, now occupied, patrolled, surrounded, divided; Vienna, home of intrigue, listening post for spies of East and West; a city seventeen miles from the watch towers on the border of Hungary, a land where no freedom existed.

Vienna, my first overseas post.

❋ ❋ ❋

In October, when our family landed at Schwechat airport outside of the city no one from our Embassy met us; Americans were not permitted to drive in this area. After World War II, Austria had been partitioned into French, British, American, and Soviet zones, each controlled by one of the powers that had defeated Hitler. Deep in the Zone under Soviet control lay Vienna and its airport. Like the country, Vienna was divided into four areas: French, British, American, and Soviet. The center of the city was an international zone, patrolled by all four powers. Passengers deplaning at Schwechat were herded onto a Soviet bus for the hour's ride into the city. At the bus depot in the central zone, Embassy friends lifted our sleeping ten-month-old from my arms, took our three-year-old's hand, and walked with us the two blocks to our hotel.

Vienna's plush hotels, once catering to the wealthy of Austria and of Europe, now housed newly arrived members of the occupying forces and sometimes their families. My husband, I, and our two children were given connecting rooms on the sixth floor of the Hotel Bristol; luxurious rooms with large curved mirrors held in gilded frames; with private railed balconies overlooking Vienna's broad Ring Street; rooms where the heated towel racks in large tiled bathrooms looked a little less luxurious holding drying diapers; rooms whose marble topped bedside tables were not accustomed to a hot plate plugged in to heat baby food jars. The Bristol's formal dining room graciously took two or three hours to serve the evening meal. After a few dressed up (and tearful) attempts, we had room service bring the meals to the bedroom. The one evening we found a sitter for the dinner hours, I dressed in my favorite long blue gown, took the elevator from the sixth floor down to the second, and then slowly descended the broad staircase leading to the lobby. A red carpet covered the center of each marble step. Where the stairs turned at the landing, I paused to see myself framed in the full sized wall mirror, my blue evening dress lovely against the mirror's edge of gold.

Across the street from the Bristol, the Soviets were housed in the Imperial Hotel. In its upper windows, I could see young children, but neither they nor their mothers ever appeared on the street. When I took our children to the nearest park, I saw no Soviet families. Viennese grandmothers of multi-layered children often stopped me, worried about my nylon snow-suited toddlers. "They'll be sick. You need a blanket," they scolded, as they tucked a blanket more closely around their swaddled babies. Later, when I began to work with children in institutions in Vienna, children orphaned or maimed by the war, I thought of these first children I had seen in Austria, the well bundled Viennese grandchildren, the secluded Soviet toddlers.

Also from our hotel balcony we could see the Soviet Army trucks driving on the Ring Street below, soldiers sitting in a U along the sides and back of an open truck. The floor of the truck and often the benches were covered with "liberated" oriental rugs. Rugs and wristwatches were the items the Soviet soldiers most wanted. I saw one boy on a truck pull up his uniform sleeve to show six wristwatches on his left arm. French, British, and American troops treated Austria as a liberated ally; their presence in the country was to help it recover from the war and regain its place in the family of nations. These three countries supported the authority of the Austrian government. By contrast, the Soviets viewed Austria as a defeated enemy, and felt that as its conquerors, they could demand reparations. As individuals, their troops could seize anything they wanted. They stole, they damaged, they raped. A helper in my home later told me, "they raped everyone, age didn't matter; even in churches, even on the floor of the main aisle. If a woman resisted she was stabbed and left there. I have two children to raise. Thank goodness, you Americans have come."

The Soviets' reputation had preceded them. In 1945 when the Viennese realized the Soviets would be the first to reach the capital, they saved their taxis by burying them in their gardens. In 1956 when the occupation ended, old taxis "grew" in several back yards of the city.

Most of the Americans in Austria were stationed in Salzburg in the western area of the country. The Embassy teenagers went there to high school, traveling back and forth through the Soviet Zone each week in a sealed train. Every Sunday the train left Vienna and every Friday it made the return trip from Salzburg. Armed U.S. military were stationed in each car and no one was allowed to stop or board the train after it left the station. With our family of preschoolers we did not worry about the train, but the Embassy directed us to be prepared at all times for a hasty evacuation. We were told to keep blankets, food, medicine and a day's supply of water in the car, to be aware of the best route out of the city, and to know always where our passports were and where our children were.

All roads out of Vienna went through the Soviet Zone. We were allowed to use only one, a route secured by agreement of the four occupying powers. The permitted road led 125 miles from Vienna to Salzburg and the West. When driving it, we checked out of the city with both Soviet and American border guards. On approaching the American Zone, we were stopped first at a Soviet checkpoint. While they examined our passports, we could see the U.S. flag flying over the American border house an eighth of a mile down the road. We tried to hide any tension we felt from our children. At the American checkpoint, our Army staffers always greeted us with warm smiles, "Welcome Home." If an expected American car took too long to reach this border, U.S. soldiers set out traveling east along the highway to look for it.

Other routes out of Vienna could be used only with advance permission from the Soviets. Hoping to see more of the country we applied three times for such permission. The first time only our one-year-old was given a pass; the second time, only our three-year-old; the third time, one parent and one child. We stopped trying.

To support the troops in Vienna, our military set up a commissary, snack bar, library, hospital, and PX, all available to Embassy members, also. The PX was in the first two floors of a building on the gurtel, the circular road around Vienna. Where the gurtel crossed Wahringerstrasse a two-story wall supported Vienna's elevated train. Steps to the train station went up from the sidewalk next to the PX door. Further down Wahringerstrasse a turn onto Boltzmangasse led to the building where the flag of the U.S. Embassy flew. The Embassy was located in the former Austrian Diplomatic Academy, an elegant building, with broad marble staircase, a building appropriate for training future diplomats of this country that was so aware of rank and appearance. Next to the Embassy two empty lots had their bombed holes hidden from view by large colorful advertising billboards, typical of those found all over the city in this year of 1952. The Boltzmangasse billboards advertised a chocolate drink, toothpaste, soap, and a store selling hosiery.

Each month, in the center of the city, a public ceremony transferred control to the next in order of the four occupying nations. Military of the incoming and outgoing teams lined up across the steps of the Hofburg Palace, flags of both nations flying, and a crowd always watching. And each month new teams of four soldiers, soldiers with no common language, patrolled the inner city, four men in each jeep.

Because in this central sector all moved freely, and because Vienna was so close to the iron curtain, the city became a center of intrigue and of spies from both sides. When the Americans learned that the man who delivered milk to our homes was being pressured by the Soviets to spy on us, the Embassy helped him leave the city. I wondered about the water inspectors who came to the house each month, but the Embassy assured me they were not spies. Despite Vienna's existing high standards, each occupying power tested the water monthly to be sure it met their own country's requirements of purity.

Within the city, diplomats were allowed to drive in all districts: the British, the French, the American, the Soviet, and, of course, in the international center. I felt safest in the central district or those under control of one of the western powers. However, Vienna's famous Prater amusement park was in the Soviet district, as was the best place to buy large amounts of ice for a reception. To pick up the ice, I would drive across the Danube into the Soviet sector, continue until I saw a large sign on the right reading "Ami Go Home." ("Ami" did not mean friend, but "American"). At the sign I turned left and drove four blocks to the icehouse, picked up the ice and returned to safety on our side of the Danube. A half-mile uphill from our home we could drive a short distance into the Vienna Woods until stopped by a very large sign marking the border of the city. "HALT! You are now entering the Soviet Zone of Austria!" it warned in four languages. On each side of its message were painted flags of the four nations. My husband and I took each other's pictures standing by the sign, but we never drove past it.

Whenever I crossed the Danube, I thought of my father. When he had learned of our assignment to Vienna, he was concerned for our safety. He had seen *The Third Man,* the Orson Welles movie, which showed the city as being full of intrigue and danger. American newspapers carried reports—unfortunately true—of bodies found floating in the Danube. My father didn't want ours to be among them.

So I never wrote to him about crossing the Danube, or that I'd been a little afraid the first time I drove there alone for ice. I did not write about spies or the evacuation precautions required by the Embassy. Rather I wrote about Vienna's restaurants, the wonderful soups, the crusty rolls, the wiener schnitzel, sachertorte, coffee (and anything else) with schlag. I wrote about the Czardisfurstin restaurant, where we were taken on our first night at this first post. The gypsy violinist played haunting music at our table; the goulyas was hot and delicious. I sat there at the corner table and knew I was in Europe. I was starting a new career. My romanticism and the good food made this our favorite restaurant. We discovered their thinner goulyas suppe made a perfect finish after an evening cocktail party. Two years later before leaving for a new assignment in Washington, we had a last dinner at the Czardisfurstin. When we asked the kind proprietor if we could take their goulyas recipe home to America with us, he listed the ingredients: "First, peel forty pounds of potatoes…"

I wrote home, too, of the music of Vienna, music we heard everywhere, in restaurants, in cafes, in parks, in department stores. The main opera was just being rebuilt—importantly the first item of rebuilding in this city. Meanwhile, operas were held at the Volks Oper, sometimes at the Theater an der Wien, where Beethoven's *Fidelio* had first been performed. I wrote about the outdoor meat and vegetable stalls, about taking our children on the miniature railroad ride through the Prater, about the day we went up in the Prater's giant ferris wheel. Then I rewrote that part, leaving out the Riesenrad (giant wheel). It had played an important and menacing role in *The Third Man*. At Christmas, I wrote about the outdoor Christkindl Markt, and about my visit to Gerngross department store on the Maria Hilfestrasse. The store when I entered it that snowy December day was filled with a song I had often heard my mother sing: "*Ihr Kinderlein Komet,*" "Oh come little children to Bethlehem's stall." To please my mother, I had learned the carol and sung it at a high school Christmas pageant. She had sat on a wooden folding chair in the school's third floor auditorium to listen. Hearing the music now, confirmed this was the right place to begin my new career. I knew my father would welcome this memory.

And, because he was always proud of my work with children, I wrote that the Embassy had asked me to become chairman of the Children's Friendship Fund, an Austro-American organization established to help children orphaned or injured during the war. I wrote about the many institutions I visited, about the help we could give them and about the many donations from the States that helped in our efforts. I did not describe the most severely maimed of the children I saw, those who would probably be hospitalized for life. Instead, I wrote of representing the Embassy in meetings with directors of the institutions and with Austrian government officials, and about being the leader of more than a hundred Austrian and American volunteers. For many of the Austrian women, this was their first experience in volunteering.

After two years we left Vienna without having seen much of eastern Austria and without a usable recipe for goulyas soup, but we carried many other things: memories of a city and a people recovering from war and occupation; memories of many brave Austrians, and of many who had agreed with or found it easier to go along with Hitler; with sure knowledge that both groups existed in the city and in the country. We left with memories of the beauty of Vienna's remaining buildings, its hills and parks, its museums, its coffee houses, even the one where I had bravely ordered my first cup of Viennese coffee. "Large, of course," I replied to the waiter. The drink was so strong, only my pride enabled me to drink it past the halfway mark. We left Vienna with a feeling for the Austro-Hungarian Empire that had once been, and of the strong remnants of that empire in the hearts of the Viennese. And we left with two healthy children and their passports.

Fifteen years later, with my husband now Deputy Chief of Mission, we returned to Vienna and found a lively city with robust citizens. We no longer passed bombed out buildings or the billboards which had hidden those empty cellars. The PX and the patrolling jeeps were gone. New taxis replaced those dug up in '56. The rebuilt opera was once again the point from which all mileage in Austria was reckoned. On New Year's Eve, dressed in tuxedo and long gown, my husband and I attended the opera's gala performance. We were accompanied by the daughter who, then three years old, had held a hand walking to the Hotel Bristol our first evening. Tonight she wore her high school prom gown.

We thought our first tour was long behind us, but our second daughter, not yet born in 1952, remembers that even fifteen years later her father and I seemed reluctant to visit the Prater; that although she could see the lights of the distant park from her bedroom window, she sensed in us an old hesitation at crossing the Danube.

It made me realize that the tension of living in an occupied city was as much a part of my memories as is my romantic feeling of that first Foreign Service post.

Broken Leg

It wasn't a simple break, and it wasn't a simple cure. To begin with, I laughed when it happened. On his first-ever afternoon of skiing, my husband took "one last trip" down the slope, and he fell. He looked so funny lying in the snow propped on one elbow, skis and legs going in two impossible directions, a half smile on his face, I skied over to take his picture. "Just one more shot and then I'll help you get up," I laughed.

"Don't move him," ordered an army ski patrol gliding to a stop at my side. "That leg may be broken." A blast on his whistle brought two GI's skiing up the hill pulling a stretcher behind them.

"We'll take care of it, Ma'am," they said; and to my husband, "Sir, we just need to see your ID card; then we'll take you down."

"The card's in my wallet in my back pocket. I'm sitting on it. I can't move to reach it." Fred's half smile disappeared.

"We have to see it before we can lift you. No ID, no stretcher."

What was the trouble with these two U.S. soldiers? I thought. How could they ask an injured man to turn over in the snow? My husband and I, then assigned to the U.S. Embassy in Vienna, were skiing in a U.S. Army Rest and Recreation Center in Germany. Such military facilities were regularly made available to members of the American Embassy. To enter this fenced and guarded recreation center we had shown our Embassy identification. We had shown ID's a second time when we were given the large dated tags conspicuously tied on each of our ski jackets, a third time when we rented these skis with a large "U.S. Army" painted prominently on their surfaces, and a fourth time when we rented the ski poles with a smaller "USA" stamped on them. Still the card must be seen once again before Fred could be put on the stretcher. "Here's mine," I said, pulling it out of my wallet.

"It must be the injured person's card. Regulations."

The stretcher-bearers rolled Fred over slightly, I reached in his pocket for the wallet, and the fallen skier could "by regulation" be taken down the slopes. The stretcher went into a waiting ambulance, which would take him across the Austrian-German border to our Military Hospital in Salzburg. I followed in our car.

The border guards waved the ambulance quickly through, but I had to stop for identification. As I waited in line, a woman knocked urgently on the car window asking me for a ride across into Austria. I knew my diplomatic license plates would get me through that tightly guarded border, but I also knew, with a pang, that I couldn't take anyone else. I always wondered what her reasons were.

At Salzburg an army doctor set the leg (afterwards I was to wonder what his real specialty was), and we were booked onto the Mozart train for the trip to Vienna, the same train Embassy high school students rode on their weekly trips between their school in Salzburg and their families in Vienna.

The train may have been good transport for high-schoolers, but it was not prepared for a patient on a stretcher. After much confusion as to how to get the stretcher into the passenger car, someone suggested pulling the train's side window down from the top. Three men stood on the station platform, lifted the stretcher up over their heads, and pushed it—with its patient—through the top of the narrowly opened window. I left our car with friends in Salzburg, and rode home on the Mozart with Fred.

At the Army Hospital in Vienna, the surgeon on duty looked at the leg and the X-rays.

"No wonder you're in pain. That's a bad break, a celery break. They set it wrong in Salzburg. We'll reset it. We'll drill a hole in your ankle, run a steel rod up to your knee. Cross rods at the top and bottom will hold it fine. The rods can stay in for life." It did not sound like a cheerful prognosis.

Fortunately for us, if not for him, there had been another broken leg at the Embassy that winter. The Ambassador's aide, who did not ski, had not wanted to decline when the Ambassador invited him for a day on the slopes. "How hard can it be to ski?" the aide joked. He never found out. At the top of the hill gathering his nerve to start down, he lit a cigarette. The process of striking the match threw him off balance, and he fell, breaking his ankle while standing still. When he heard about the steel rods for Fred, he came right over. "Don't let them do it. Let me see if you can go to Dr. Bohler. He's the best there is and he fixed my leg."

So the following day we found ourselves again in an ambulance, this time en route to Vienna's Unfall Krankenhaus (accident hospital). We entered into a long, crowded corridor; both sides were lined with patients on stretchers, in wheel chairs, or leaning against the walls. Most had a family member with them. We could feel the expectancy as Dr. Bohler approached. My first thought when I saw him coming down the hospital corridor was that he looked like God, like God as pictured in children's books of Bible stories, or the God in a Hollywood epic of creation. Everything about him seemed larger that life: his height, intensified by a long white lab coat, a large head, large hands. His white hair and white beard encircled a calm face.

The doctor moved along the hallway stopping briefly by each patient, listening to the need, prescribing treatment, and indicating which cases he would see personally. He paused at my husband's stretcher, glanced through the report we had brought and nodded, "Ja." He walked on. I felt filled with relief. Here was someone who would know what to do.

Dr. Bohler did know what to do and he did wonders. With those large hands he manipulated the bones and then put Fred in a long hip to toe cast. It stayed on for nine months. We made many visits to the Unfall Krankenhaus during those months and we came to have great respect for Dr. Bohler's skill and his knowledge.

For Fred's convalescence we put a bed in the living room of our Vienna home. He could have meetings there and he was near the dining room and near the sunny terrace. There was only one problem. The first floor lavatory was a tiny room off the stone floored front hall—a room so small not even a sink could fit in it, but had been placed nearby in the alcove where guests hung their coats. My husband and his cast could not fit in such a room and shut the door; the cast-covered leg must extend out into the hall. Toes of the extended leg pointed toward the front door, the living room, and the stairs to the second floor. Just west of his ankle was the door to the kitchen. Whenever Fred needed to use the facilities, life in the household came to a halt. We emptied the front hall and the living room of people, no one could go up or down stairs, and we shut the door leading to the kitchen.

I'm sure this complex process hastened the time when he became able to go upstairs by a backward sitting down technique, stair to stair. Not easy, but it did give him a little more privacy.

In a few weeks he was able to return to his Embassy office. I drove him down in the morning and he liked to take the streetcar home. Vienna's #38 carline left a block from the Embassy and came directly to the foot of our hill in the suburb of Grinzing. I waited at the end of the carline.

It seemed a satisfactory arrangement until the day the lady who helped in our house came to me in some distress. She had been told by other household workers in the neighborhood that her employer was riding home in the third car of the streetcar. This lowered her standing in the community, she said. All Vienna trams had at least three cars. Important people—those in business suits and carrying briefcases—crowded into the front car. Often they had to stand. Medium people—a baker, a suburban mother and children—would ride in car two where one might or might not find a seat. Only laborers rode in the third car. The third car always had seats. I reported to Fred Maria's concern about her prestige but he said she would just have to endure the shame. No way would he stand with a thigh high cast and his briefcase in the first car, when he could sit with his leg spread out on a seat in car three.

Maria might have felt better if she had known Fred would one day reach the rank of Ambassador, as would our leg-saving friend who fell down lighting his cigarette at the top of the ski slope. Dr. Bohler, I think, would just be pleased that both of his patients have gone through over forty years with strong and pain free legs. Today my husband is not sure which leg was broken.

Dr. Bohler might also be pleased to know we remember and follow his advice. A phrase he used at each Unfall Krankenhaus visit has become part of our family lore. His firm instruction during and at the end of each examination was, "Die Zehen bewegen." "Move the toes." We used the phrase when Fred had back surgery and later knee surgery. We use it when anyone in the family is bedridden. "Die Zehen bewegen." "Move the toes." Keep the circulation going.

Himmelstrasse

During our first tour in Vienna we lived on the "Street of Heaven." Himmelstrasse rose sharply from the Viennese suburb of Grinzing. It climbed past our house up to the Vienna Woods, and, one assumes, to heaven beyond. The slope was so steep that in winter we could put on skis at our front gate and glide directly down to the village below. On summer Sunday mornings Himmelstrasse was filled with Austrians walking up to the Wienerwald, baskets of lunch on their arms. Each week, in dirndls and lederhosen, children and adults climbed upwards. In the evening, singing voices preceded and followed the picnickers as they descended to Grinzing.

Our family came to Himmelstrasse by default. In the housing shortage of post World War II Vienna, newly arrived Embassy personnel stayed in the Bristol Hotel until they had enough "points" to be given housing. Points were earned by length of stay in the hotel, the number in your family, your representational or entertainment needs. An Embassy housing committee supervised assignments. When the Himmelstrasse house became available, we had reached number three on the waiting list. Fortunately for us, families one and two turned it down. Family one thought the chalet type house not formal enough for their needs, and family two feared the steep hill would be impassable in Austria's winters. Our family of father, mother, a three-year-old and a ten-month-old had just spent three months in connecting hotel rooms. We had been fixing the baby's food on a hot plate, and drying his diapers on the towel heating rack in the bathroom; they hung there twenty-four hours a day. A lovely chalet with kitchen, laundry space and four bedrooms looked very inviting to us. We couldn't worry about the snow on the street.

Besides, as my husband pointed out, the Commanding General

of U.S. Forces, Austria lived on Himmelstrasse five houses below ours. We felt sure the army would keep the road open at least that far. Our Embassy Marines lived three houses down, and we knew they would get home somehow. So would we.

In early December we moved in. The house was white stucco, its gothic arched front door made of strips of curved wood. A terrace on one side faced south, and beyond the apricot trees in that yard was a fenced vegetable garden. Two bedrooms opened onto a balcony overlooking the hilled vineyards of Grinzing to the right and the city of Vienna to the left. The balcony's carved wood railing looked like an Alpine scene in Heidi movies or all the Austrian chalets we had seen in travel books. For our first tour in the Foreign Service, it couldn't have been more Austrian or more romantic.

The Himmelstrasse home had been requisitioned. Properties owned by prominent Nazis had been confiscated by the Austrian government at the end of the war. That government let them be used as needed by the four occupying powers: France, England, the Soviet Union, the United States. We were the only power that paid rent for such use. Return of the property in good condition had been assured, and owners were given permission to visit a building to see if it was being given good care. In our case, the wealthy owners lived in another home they owned further up Himmelstrasse. I know they were concerned about the large ornate Biedermeyer dining room set they had left in the house, and they did not like the dull green covering the Army had put on their built-in upholstered furniture in the living room (nor did I), but they could see the house was being kept up and cared for.

At the end of his second visit, the owner asked me if our family would trade houses with him and use the one further up the hill. "It has many closets," he tried to persuade me. "I know Americans like closets." Ours had only those in the master bedroom.

I remember thinking this scene is not right. I cannot understand how this decision is left to me, a thirty-year old first tour wife. I did not want to move. We would move often enough in a Foreign Service life; I didn't want a mid-tour move, too. Also, our family had settled comfortably into the house and garden. Still, I thought, it must be hard to want to be back in your own home instead of having foreigners living there. I reminded myself this man must have been a leading Nazi for his property to be confiscated, but I wondered, "Was he really?" As my head whirled, the conversation continued calmly. Suddenly my decision was made easy. Herr ... drew from his jacket pocket some prints of a painting that had been made of the house. "I'd like to give you one of these," he said. "One summer a few years ago, we had a very large and happy party here in the garden. An artist who was present painted the picture as a thank you remembrance of the day." Reproduced on 4 x 6 cards, the painting was as lovely as the house. I looked at it carefully, and my heart froze. In the lower left corner was the date of the "happy party": June 6, 1944. June 6, D-Day. While these high Nazis had been partying in the summer sun, my brother and other Americans had been wading ashore in Northern France, many of them to be killed by bullets from this man's compatriots. "Thank you for coming," I said, declining the card. "The Embassy will be in touch with you." I still remember the clutch in my chest when I read the date.

And so we stayed on for two years at Himmelstrasse. Sue had her tonsils out while we lived there; Dickie had the first fever convulsion I had ever seen; Fred broke his leg and spent months in a long, high cast. We became close friends with our Austrian pediatrician and surgeon.

For the first time in our lives we had live-in household help, and even a seamstress who came for a week one fall. We had one helper who stole, another who had serious mental problems—how I sped home to the children the day I learned that! The husband of our favorite helper was a construction worker helping rebuild the State Opera after its war damage, a position that far outranked any other construction job in Vienna.

During our two years there, the children played and grew in the garden. We picked our own strawberries, raspberries, and broccoli. An Austrian friend helped me make delicious jam from the laden apricot trees, and we sent bags of fruit in to the Embassy. The children lost a goldfish, who was buried in the garden, and two parakeets—we hoped they flew to the Vienna Woods. I took piano lessons; Fred studied the zither with a member of the Vienna Philharmonic, the best part of each lesson being when the teacher opened with a demonstration, often the theme from the *Third Man* movie. In December we took the children to the Christkindl Market, a festive outdoor Christmas bazaar. Late one Christmas Eve, Fred and I bought our Christmas tree at a tiny square in snowy downtown Vienna. Three days earlier we had hired sleighs to bring guests up our hill for a party.

We lived always with the awareness that we were in a city deep in the Soviet-controlled Zone of Austria, that our reluctant landlord lived just up the hill, that he was not the only Austrian who had welcomed the Nazis. We knew that we were guaranteed only one "safe" road out to the west and we memorized the route. We always knew exactly where our passports were and exactly where our children were. In case of a hasty evacuation anything else could be left behind.

Despite the tensions, our two years in Austria were happy ones. We laughed a lot and we learned a lot. Just before leaving, we held a farewell party in the garden, the same garden where ten years earlier the Nazis had held their "very large and happy party." The day we left, a rainbow spread over the garden. We didn't know it meant we'd be back.

NEW ZEALAND 1960-62

We cross the Pacific

Stopover in Fiji

Fiji: warm gentle breezes, swaying palm trees, sunny beaches, endless light blue sky overall. After July in too-hot Washington, a week in too-cold Los Angeles, and with an unknown New Zealand ahead, our children asked, "Couldn't we just stay here in Fiji?"

We did stay for three relaxing days. We swam and rested at the beach. We toured the island. We visited a Fijian village with its houses on stilts, and a friendly chieftain who invited us to climb up the ladder entrance to his one room home. Single beds along the side walls and a table at the far end were inviting, as was his pleasant manner. In the evening we ate in the hotel's dining room, first dressing for dinner in this British outpost. We were served by tall barefoot Fijian waiters, their crisp white shirts tucked into white skirts cut in deep vees where they ended at mid calf.

On the island tour we stopped at a small shop for souvenirs of our visit. Our two older children picked out typical Fijian gifts: pictures of the island, gifts made of shells or native plants, or items labeled Fiji in colorful raffia letters. Our youngest chose a small fold-over blue plastic purse with a gold clasp. The shopkeeper and her parents tempted her with typical objects that would say we'd been in Fiji, but the blue purse is what she wanted and that is what she carried out of the store. Today, years later, the typical souvenirs are lost and long forgotten. The bright blue purse is in my younger daughter's upper drawer. It says both Fiji and determination.

Fiji was our last stop on our way to our new assignment. We had broken the fifteen-hour trip into three segments. The first leg had taken us from Washington to California, to San Francisco and then on to Los Angeles where we spent a promised day at Disneyland. Disneyland in 1960 was uncrowded and pleasant, the cleanest amusement park I had ever seen. We rode the cars over the skies of Mary Poppins' London. Our four-year-old had her picture taken with Mickey and Minnie. Also in LA that July, the Democratic National convention was meeting. Sue, at eleven, was old enough to be excited at this, and we walked over to headquarters hotel to sense the flavor of the gathering. Many weeks later we would vote absentee and gather to await election results at the Ambassador's Residence in Wellington. Election Day was always one of the days I felt most homesick for America.

We had planned the stop in Fiji to help us adjust to the many time zones we would pass through between Boston and Wellington; also to prepare for the change of seasons. From this island, our final flight would carry us across the equator into the southern hemisphere and winter. In preparation for the change we had sent one of our three allowed airfreight trunks to the airport hotel in Fiji. The trunk held winter outfits for each of the five in our family: warm clothes for our arrival and beginning in New Zealand. Each child and adult had one "good" outfit, a travel outfit for the final leg of our trip, an every day something (play clothes for the children, casual wear for my husband and myself). With each outfit I had packed appropriate shoes, coat, hat, jacket, accessories. When we left Fiji for Wellington we would be appropriately dressed, and for a week or so, with laundry, we could face what lay ahead.

In Washington's May of 80 degrees the packing of winter clothes had seemed odd. Finding winter clothes had been even more of a challenge. During the preceding stateside winter, we had not known we would be moving to New Zealand in the summer. By April, when we did know, stores carried only summer clothes. Finally, in the small city of North Adams, Massachusetts, near my father's home, an independent storekeeper who knew us, said, "Dorothy, let me go look in our basement to see if I have winter pajamas for the children." He found them in sizes five, ten, and twelve. As I was to write to him later, we thought of him warmly in our unheated home in Wellington. Finally, the necessities had been gathered and by the deadline for shipping, the trunk went off. We hoped it would be waiting in Fiji.

The trunk was there. For a short time it was the only luggage we had.

The plane that deposited the five of us on the island was about to take off for its next destination when we realized our suitcases had not been unloaded. As there had been no stops since leaving California, we asked the crew to look again. They obliged pleasantly, but returned to say there were no suitcases left on board. With minutes until departure time, my husband said, "Let me look," and climbed into the luggage section of the plane. As I stood watching at the airport window with our three children, his disappearance into the plane seemed very long. Seconds flew into minutes, and I found myself considering what I would do if the plane took off with him in it. Should I stay in Fiji with the children until he returned or should we go on to New Zealand and meet him there? In what seemed a very long time, he crawled out of the plane to say that he had found the bags. Two handlers immediately went on and carried out the luggage. Fred was barely on the ground when the plane taxied for takeoff. For my husband, the first thought when he hears "Fiji" is the innards of an overseas plane.

For me, it is the ironing room at the Nandi Hotel. The airport hotel was made up of several small one-story buildings. One held a reception lounge for waiting travelers; a second housed the large dining room. We walked across a low grass covered hill to the bedroom building. Our three small rooms were next to each other. When our children saw that one room held double decker beds, they were sure this was a sign they were supposed to stay. In the largest room waited our trunk. The winter clothing was safely inside, well creased by its two month journey.

The young woman who cleaned our room did not iron, but led me to the laundry room in yet another small building. She watched with interest as I pressed our clothes for the trip across the last part of the Pacific. Few tourists stayed at this airport hotel. Probably even fewer spent their time ironing woolen clothes.

After three days it was time to leave the island. We packed away our shorts and sandals and put on the newly ironed woolens. We looked hot, but, in a suitably wintry way, stylish to arrive in our new country.

I wore a green wool dress, my black coat and my favorite small black hat. We knew New Zealand would be cold. At Auckland we changed planes for Wellington where we met not only cold, but also darkness, strong winds, heavy rain slashing sideways. New Englanders would call it a northeaster.

Getting off the plane in Wellington, I put my purse and carry-on bag in my left hand so my right could hold on to my hat. Our four-year-old leaned against me in the dark and reached up her hand. Between a hat and a lonely child there was no choice. I took Barbara's hand; the hat was gusted out of sight. A raincoated New Zealand stewardess hurried us across the tarmac into the terminal. I entered the airport building, hatless, with dripping hair, clothing less ironed than when we left Fiji. As we greeted the Embassy officials there to welcome us, a very wet stewardess came up to us holding out my hat. "I chased it to the end of the field. I'm afraid its been somewhat squashed," she apologized as she handed me the dripping object. Her kind act on a cold wet night warmed my heart.

I Meet The Press

My husband and I spent our first Saturday in New Zealand washing windows at an elementary school. It is not because we are so enthusiastic about clean windows that we travel half way around the globe to find a needy pane of glass. It was my first newspaper headline that put us up on ladders, rags and Windex in hand.

On Tuesday we had arrived in New Zealand to begin our tour at the U.S. Embassy. On Wednesday, as the wife of the new Economics Officer, I had been interviewed for my, "First Impressions of New Zealand." In answer to a question about whether my teacher training was helpful in parenting, I had laughed and said, "Oh, it's so different with your own children."

On Thursday the paper carrying the interview was delivered to our home. I was eagerly skimming its pages when the headline stopped me: "Teacher says Training of No Help at All."

My heart sank. There could be no mistaking the teacher being quoted. Directly over the article was a clear picture of me with our three children—three children who would soon be attending New Zealand's public schools. What would their teachers think of my attitude? What would the Ambassador think of this new member of the Embassy? I phoned my husband.

"Did you see the *Gazette*?" I asked.

"Yes, not great, is it?"

"What did the Ambassador say?"

"Staff meeting's in ten minutes. I'll let you know."

For an hour I busied myself with trivia until Fred called back.

"Everyone here says not to be worried. That paper prides itself on writing startling headlines, and New Zealanders are always making fun of their schools. They'll think it's funny. Net judgment here is it's a plus."

I felt relieved that the Embassy viewed it as not serious, but it was far from a plus for me. Education is my profession, and laughing at schools or teachers is not something I do. It is certainly not the way I wish to be introduced to a new community. When Fred and I learned that our children's school-to-be was having a Home and School Association (PTA) cleanup on the coming Saturday—with teachers and parents helping— we felt we had better be there.

In my next New Zealand press encounter, the headline was more favorable, even kind: "American Embassy wife addresses conference in Palmerston North. Mrs. Irving speaks on 'Life in America.'" When I think of what the paper might have written, I was grateful. "Mrs. Irving obviously nervous in speech to large audience." I certainly was. In that first speech I felt the whole reputation of America resting on my inexperienced shoulders. The burden grew even heavier when I saw that my words were being recorded. Or a headline might have read, "Mrs. Irving eats little New Zealand food at luncheon in her honor." Of course, I ate little. The Chinese Ambassador had spoken before lunch. My speech was after lunch. I was so nervous it was hard to swallow anything.

After the Palmerston North experience, I became more relaxed about public speaking. Soon, whenever the Embassy received a request for a speaker on "America," I was usually the person sent.

Our final New Zealand interview came when we were leaving the country. Once again a cameraman came to the house to photograph our family, this time all five of us. Sue and Rick were in their local school uniforms, Sue, in a Hutt Valley High navy "gym" or jumper; Rick, in his school's gray sweater, shorts, knee socks and school tie. Barbara wore a plaid dress, but no smile. The photographer (perhaps a parent himself?) was sensitive enough to realize she was trying to hide her missing front tooth. He persuaded her, "Barbara, if you smile, I promise to fix the picture in the paper so it looks as if all your teeth are there." She smiled, and he fixed. As an extra kindness the paper sent us a copy of the untouched photo. It hangs in our den. The older two are in their school uniforms; Barbara is smiling with a gap in her mouth. It's one of our favorites.

Another favorite Foreign Service picture is one from Jamaica, many years later. While visiting a nursery school, I had knelt down to let a little girl put a homemade necklace around my neck. The boy next to her was so amused at the sight of this grownup kneeling down to his eye level, he had to hug himself to hold in his giggles. The photographer caught the moment just before the giggles burst out.

After Jamaican papers ran pictures of me dedicating a playground, visiting a literacy center, giving out prizes at a graduation, opening a flower show, giving a speech, the largest daily paper sent a photographer to accompany me through a "typical day." He took pictures as I chose vegetables in the local market, taught at the Rastafarian preschool, met at the Ministry of Education with Peace Corps teachers, welcomed a new Embassy wife with a cup of tea, worked in my garden, greeted government officials at dinner. "Is it always like this?" the cameraman asked at the end of that long hot day. It always was.

One day on a visit to a remote Jamaican school I was welcomed with the excited greeting, "Mrs. Irving, we were just reading about you in our *Weekly Readers*." No one had alerted me to this publication, but I knew enough about Jamaican politics to know that without the approval of the Prime Minister's wife, a political figure in her own right, I would not have appeared in this country-wide paper for children. I was delighted that such a friendly article would be going into homes all over Jamaica. The teacher in me was particularly delighted.

Throughout our career, both pro- and anti-American newspapers were friendly. Except for that first New Zealand piece, they carried headlines that I, my husband, and the Department of State could be happy about. All reflected efforts of an American abroad, trying to increase understanding of her country and trying to reach as many groups as possible in the country in which she was living.

This continued in Iceland. Of many articles during our four years there, I treasure two favorites. The first, a page-long write-up, showed a picture of me seated in my living room reading a large volume of *Njala*, Iceland's most beloved saga, a picture that could win many friends in that literate country. Because it appeared in the paper not usually pro-American, the article was doubly welcomed.

The second was our farewell interview. After four years we were about to leave Iceland, and a reporter had come to the Residence to interview me and my husband. We spoke of many things including our enjoyment of our years in Reykjavík. The reporter asked if we had minded the Icelandic weather. My husband replied that although it did sometimes rain in Iceland (many said a part of three hundred and thirty days in the year), I liked the country so much I always spoke of it as constantly sunny. My husband said he thought I even believed that to be true. The reporter laughed. In leaving he asked my husband if he had not been a diplomat, what other career might he have liked. Without a moment's hesitation, Fred answered him honestly.

"I always wanted to be a plumber," he replied.

"A plumber! Why did you want to do that?"

"I always thought it must be very satisfying to be able to fix a faulty drain so that the water could now go gurgle, gurgle down it."

As the reporter wrote in his article. "With that, your reporter went laughingly into the morning sunshine—the sunshine Mrs. Irving knew was always there; and he smiled at the thought that Ambassador Irving might have made as good a plumber as he was an Ambassador."

Mr. Thwaites

At four-thirty I began to be nervous. At six o'clock we were expecting eighty guests—seventy of whom I had not yet met—for the first reception we would give in New Zealand. Our house was ready: fresh flowers arranged, furniture moved to make room, serving trays ready on the kitchen cupboard. EMPTY serving trays. There was no food and no sign of food preparation. What would we offer our guests?

I began to think creatively. Our high school daughter and I were handy at whipping up things in the kitchen. During our Foreign Service career, Susan had often helped serve at buffets and receptions, and she did it well. Could we rise to this one-hour-to-go situation?

I began to wonder about Mr. Thwaites, the caterer who had been so highly recommended. Was he, despite his reputation, not reliable? Had he possibly been confused about the date?

I remembered how impressed I had been when he came to our home to discuss the upcoming party. We considered the number of guests, types of food, and costs. Mr. Thwaites was obviously a professional who took pride in his work. "I like to start with something very light followed by a fish course. Later we will pass the vegetables and the hot hors d'oeuvres with meat. Still later, the sweets and, finally, some small puffs with cheese. A reception should be like a well-planned meal. If your American Ambassador is coming we should include some New Zealand oysters. You know he likes these." (Around the world, catering and serving staffs come to know the tastes of the current personnel at all the embassies. During our tour in Iceland, such staffs knew my husband and I drank only soda water. Whenever we entered a reception, a tray soon appeared holding two tall glasses with soda water and a slice of lemon.) In New Zealand, Mr. Thwaites knew the tastes of his clientele.

On that preparatory visit, he had wanted to see our kitchen equipment and layout. "My staff will prepare everything at headquarters and bring it here ready to serve. We will want to use your oven to heat the warm food, and these cupboards for arranging trays. We'll bring ice and glasses and everything you will need."

We agreed on the menu and verified the date. I let him decide how many bites of food, how many waiters and glasses would be needed. For this first party I preferred to rely on his experience. He was familiar with the habits of his countrymen.

This party I awaited so nervously had been a challenge since its beginning. Our family had been at the Embassy in New Zealand less than a month and were still learning our way around the shops and discovering what foods were available in this new country. We would have preferred to wait a few more weeks before scheduling our debut social event. However, the Embassy had received word that Ezra Taft Benson, U.S. Secretary of Agriculture, would be visiting the country. Since the Embassy's Agricultural Attaché was on home leave, the responsibility for hosting Secretary Benson's trip fell to the Economics Officer, my husband. He needed to arrange tours of agricultural facilities, meetings with New Zealand officials, and some kind of welcoming social event for the Washington visitors.

We considered having a small dinner for them, perhaps six or eight tables of six. In this house, still new to us, we devised a clever way of measuring how many tables our first floor could hold. From Embassy friends we borrowed a round table top—the kind that enlarges a card table to seat six—and we placed it on the floor at the far end of our living room. My husband, I, and our three children clasped hands in a circle around the tabletop stretching to leave enough room for six imagined chairs. Barbara, at four, couldn't stretch her arms as far as Rick at nine and Susan at eleven, but she helped. We marked the outer edge of table one. We estimated the space for waiters, and moved to lay out table two. When table three came too close to the living room door, we canceled plans for a dinner. I returned the top to our friends. "It has to be a reception," I told them. "We'll need a caterer. Who is good?" The answer from them and from everyone at the Embassy was, "Mr. Thwaites."

It was that very Mr. Thwaites I now awaited. (Where was he?)

Finally, at ten minutes to five a very large white van backed up our long driveway and parked by the kitchen door. Out stepped Mr. Thwaites and four other men, all in shirtsleeves. The bustle began. One man carried in large cartons, one unpacked, wiped and arranged glasses, one fixed a corner to serve as a bar, and a last placed food on trays ready to refrigerate or heat. I glanced at the activity in the kitchen and left them to their tasks. At ten of six, Mr. Thwaites, now in white jacket, came into the living room to say that everything was ready. Had I any last minute wishes?

"We found some very nice oysters for your Ambassador," he added with pride. "I'll wait to serve them until he arrives. Meanwhile, may I give the children a bit of something hot?" I learned later that he had given them several bits during the party. "Every time we went into the kitchen we got something good," said Rick, "and he let us help, too."

Mr. Thwaites not only won our children's hearts, he won ours, too. The food was delicious. The Ambassador did enjoy the oysters, as did everyone. The evening went well. We met the leaders of New Zealand's agricultural community, many of whom became friends. The head of the farmers' group so enjoyed seeing our children help with coats and serving, that he invited our family to come to their farm for a picnic their association was having. Susan, Rick, and Barbara still remember that pleasant day, the baby calf, the swing on the tree, the woman who gave them extra desserts. It's a favorite New Zealand memory.

As for Mr. Thwaites, I never doubted him again. And I knew never to look at the clock as a party hour drew near. When planning any event that needed catering, I phoned him first to learn his schedule. Then I invited the guests.

I was amused a few years later when another family accorded our daughter this same role in their entertaining. Susan responded to a request on her college bulletin board: "Student needed to serve at buffet dinner in faculty home." "It's much better than baby sitting," she wrote us, "and I get a delicious meal, too." After her first evening there, whenever the professor's family hoped to have a dinner, they first phoned Susan for her free dates. At college graduation, they invited our family to tea to thank us. "Now that she's graduated we don't know how we'll entertain. We always knew that when Susan was here it would be all right." I smiled as I recognized the feeling.

Fire!

The morning our house burned I was not at home. It had been my turn to help at our daughter's nursery school. This school was not the best one in our new town of Lower Hutt, New Zealand, but when I applied to the one most highly recommended, I had been turned down.

"You hope to enroll your daughter for this year, Mrs. Irving? Parents register their children at birth to save a place with us." declared the haughty director.

"At her birth, I could not have predicted that Barbara would be here in New Zealand when she was the age to start school." I replied with controlled anger.

"That is your misfortune. We are full."

Barbara's need for playmates was so strong that I chose the best available from those schools with openings, and it was here she and I had spent our morning. In the States, either as a teacher or a participating parent, I looked forward to nursery school mornings, but this school was so mediocre, it was hard to be enthused. I came home tired.

As we turned into our long driveway, I noticed something strange about the house. The one-story den extending to the left was dark. Four casement windows on opposite sides usually filled the room with light—the sun pouring in one side in the morning and the other in the afternoon. Today there was no light. "I must have forgotten to open the drapes," I thought. As I drove nearer, I saw that the curtains were open. It was dense smoke that blocked light from the windows. Fire? My heart thumped.

I pulled the car to the top of the drive. "Barbara, you wait here in the car. I'll go in and look. I'll be right back." I tried to sound calm. With an awareness of my responsibility for the government-owned property we lived in, I went inside to turn off the electricity. I don't know what I thought that would do.

As I stood by the kitchen fuse box, a quick glance around showed flames and smoke coming out of the waist-high paneling in the hall and along the stairs. Rushing back to the car, I took Barbara and hurried to our neighbor's home to phone the Fire Department and my husband at the Embassy. A family tradition harking back to my grandmother said you never phone your husband at work, and never, never call him out of a meeting. "He's in a meeting with the chargé d'affaires," his secretary answered. My grandmother would have known when traditions should end. "You'll have to call him out. Our house is on fire."

An Embassy member drove Fred the ten miles to the house in less than that many minutes. The Fire Department had already arrived. I had met them on the lawn to tell them where I had seen flames and to assure them no one was inside. Our neighbors waited outside with us near the long white fire hose stretched across our yard.

When the firemen had finished their work, we went in the house to see the damage. There was some from the flames: charred wood in the kitchen, the hall, and up the stairs. But the greater damage was caused by soot from burning furnace oil. Two days earlier all of our things from the States had arrived and we had been in the midst of unpacking and putting them away. Dishes were stacked on the dining room table, knickknacks, on the den desk; clothes lay on an extra bed; pictures leaned against walls where they might be hung; dolls, books, toys were in open boxes upstairs. All were covered with soot. In our bedroom, the room furthest from the flames, I lifted down a hat in the closet. It left on the shelf an exact circle of its shape. The soot permeated drawers, too. A knife looked clean, but when it cut bread, the bread had a thin black layer. We gladly accepted the invitation of friends to spend the night with them.

Throughout the day of the fire, I had stayed calm, helping Barbara, welcoming our two older children home from school, moving clothes to our friends, and giving firemen any information I could. Later several of the firefighters spoke of how "steady" Mrs. Irving had been during the fire.

It was good they did not see me the following day. A painter came to see what repairs would be needed. I walked with him through each room. Upstairs, while showing him Barbara's room, I lifted a doll off the bookcase. When I saw its perfect outline left behind, I sat down on her bed and cried. I remember the painter was nice about it.

In the days following the fire there were some laughable incidents. Sitting at a Home and School Association meeting that week, I whispered to Fred, "This school smells smoky. It must be in our noses."

"It's not our noses or the school," he replied. "It's our clothes." He was right. Although most of our clothing was at the cleaners, we had kept out what we thought were the least smelly things for immediate wear.

A few evenings later, a New Zealand friend offered, "Dorothy, let me lend you a coat. I won't miss it. I have coats to burn." We laughed together. "That's the only kind I can borrow." I accepted.

The fire had started from an explosion in the furnace that was the "central heating" of our house. New Zealanders prided themselves on not needing central heating. Even new homes omitted it. Rainy, thirty-degree days were not comfortable, but it was a matter of character to survive them. At any dinner party, we, as Americans, were put closest to the fireplace, so that at least one side of us was warm. I learned early on to avoid winter trips to anyone's powder room. Such a room was invariably unheated and down a long unheated hall.

In our home, the central heater earned its name by location. Exactly in the center of this basement-less house, there was a hole under the hall floor, where the furnace sat. I have no idea how it was put there or how it was serviced. Apparently, this one had not been serviced enough. There had been trouble with it almost every year before we arrived, but the Embassy official in charge had thought it did not merit funds from his closely watched budget. Now his cost would be even higher. It was clear the fire had been caused by an explosion from this heater.

When the furnace had functioned properly, heat entered the house through a four-foot square iron grill in the floor directly over it. This was the warmest spot in the house. Our children came home for lunch from their unheated school and stood on the grill to warm up. Soon all their shoes had grid patterns on the soles. (So did mine.) The first floor telephone was in a built-in nook by this grill. The location made for short phone conversations when a blast of hot air was erupting under one's feet. Rooms in the house were comfortable or freezing in direct proportion to the turns, walls, or distance between them and this central hot blast. Our bedroom, up the stairs and down a long hall, was rarely warm.

When we learned the cause of the fire, and thought of the location of our rooms, we were overwhelmed with gratitude that none of us had been at home when the explosion occurred—especially that we had not been a family asleep at the time. Barbara's room was right at the top of the stairs, almost over the heater; Rick's room was across the hall from hers. Next to them, Susan slept, and then down a hall about thirty feet long was our bedroom. We didn't want to think how thick the smoke in the children's bedrooms would have become before it reached our room with enough density to waken us. It was too scary to consider.

As I look back on the New Zealand fire, I remember the long white hose on the lawn outside, and the black soot everywhere inside. The two words I always associate with that day remain connected in my mind: "Fire" and "Beauty." "Beauty" in New Zealand was often used as an adjective: "That's a beauty flower." On this day it might have been a noun, too. The afternoon of the fire, Barbara was going to a friend's birthday party. I shook out her favorite light blue party dress with its tiered ruffled skirt. Wearing white socks, black patent leather shoes, the lovely blue dress, and carrying her gift-wrapped birthday present in her hand, she walked proudly down those charred stairs.

"I am beauty," she said.

Oyster Crackers?

We put the forty-seven boxes of oyster crackers on shelves we built into the shower stall. There didn't seem to be any other place. The house in New Zealand had only one closet—upstairs—no attic, no basement, no nook or cranny where a shelf could be put.

"That first floor shower is the only place I can see," said my husband, and he constructed four wooden shelves there. Next to the oyster crackers stood the forty-six cans of Campbell's onion soup (two cans had been used in a family recipe the day they arrived). Eleven boxes of Tootsie Rolls, and twelve boxes each of mixes of brownies and Ten-B-Low Ice Cream were on the bottom shelves. I thought of photographing the display and labeling it HOMESICK.

When we lived abroad, homesickness came in many ways. Sometimes, an American movie would do it—not the plot, the stars or the music, but the scenes of daily life, the glimpses of an American city, of the American countryside, of all those people speaking American English. No matter how much we liked our temporary home abroad, no matter how much we believed in the importance of our work there, to quote the Scottish song, wherever we lived was "not the hills of home."

Often, a favorite food would become part of what we missed. Never had the gustatory longing been as strong as it was in New Zealand. New Zealand had good food, clean and safe, excellent British crackers—I still buy Hunt's Cream Crackers whenever I see them—and the country had a canned Scotch Broth we all liked. Fresh meat and a limited supply of fruits and vegetables were available. It was not that we "needed" any food from home. What we needed was comforting and nurturing.

Our first year in New Zealand had been difficult. For nine months we had lived out of a trunk and five suitcases, awaiting the arrival of the rest of our clothing, of our books, pictures, toys, bikes, dishes—everything to supplement the basic furniture that came with the house. The day after our shipment arrived, we had a fire in the house so extensive we had to move out for three months while repairs were made. In that first year, our three children had two appendectomies (one, an emergency), one tonsillectomy, and a serious case of measles. Their schools were disappointing at best, frightening at worst. One teacher counted a day wasted if no student was caned for misbehavior. In our daughter's high school, since girls were too old to be caned by male teachers, the accepted method of discipline was to pull the student's hair. At home, our kindergartner played school with a patent leather belt curled on the desk next to her crayons. "That's the strap," she answered my question. "It's used when children are bad at school."

It was the stress of that first year that made our longing for familiar food so great. Since our parents couldn't bring us my mother's turkey dressing or my mother-in-law's chicken soup, since we couldn't fly home to eat, we decided to order foods that would bring home to us. The oyster crackers were for my husband and me; the brownies for the children, and the Ten-B-Low for all of us. New Zealand did not sell ice cream in the winter.

From a food wholesaler in the States, Americans abroad could order canned and packaged food by the case. Embassy families often shared or split a case two or three ways. No one else had signed up for oyster crackers, and we had not realized a case meant forty-eight boxes of the salty delicacies. Still, we thought, once the food is here, others will want a few boxes. Not so. We had all forty-eight to ourselves, a pile that diminished ever more gradually as our second year passed. At least, we comforted ourselves, we were not so foolish as our co-worker who had ordered a case of Lipton's tea—sent to British New Zealand! Soon the Tootsie Rolls, brownies and ice cream disappeared. The onion soup moved more slowly. When we learned we were due to be transferred home, fourteen cans of it still stood on the shower shelf. That favorite family recipe we had welcomed so eagerly when the food arrived was now our menu every other night until we left. We were back in Washington a long time before we cooked it again—or before we bought oyster crackers.

Seven years after the oyster cracker purchase our family was stationed in Austria, and we recognized a similar longing for stateside foods in a group of eleven-year-old American boys who came to our Vienna house for lunch. The boys were spending a year studying at Melk, Austria, and had come to the capital for the day. As they walked to the kitchen to help me get dessert, they passed the open door of our food pantry.

"Look, Campbell's soups!" exclaimed one, discernible longing in his voice. He stopped in front of the open pantry. The others crowded in to look at and touch those familiar red and white cans. Some of the world's best soups are made in Austria: suppenhuhn, suppe mit knudeln, gulyassuppe, and on and on. What these eleven-year-old boys saw on my pantry shelf was not food. It was home. Each boy returned to school carrying two cans of soup. I never asked if they shared them with their school's cook, heated them in their rooms for a special snack, or just placed a can on bookshelf or desk as a tangible link with the United States. I wonder where those boys are now and if they remember their visit. I wonder what they miss from Austria, and if they buy Campbell's soups.

ALONG THE WAY

Our Children

Foreign Service Children

What is it like for children growing up in the Foreign Service? Is it a challenge or a treat? The questions come from old and new friends. Did your three like it? Did they decide to follow the same career?

Trying to answer honestly, I looked back over our children's Foreign Service years.

I remembered our first tour in Vienna. With our children, then ten months and three years old, we lived in a hotel for three months awaiting housing. My husband and I had chosen this career, but we were always aware that the children had had no say in it. I felt especially sorry for the three-year-old, accustomed to the freedom of an American back yard, and now confined to a hotel room. To "make it up to her" I tried to overlook misbehavior I would have corrected at home. After several days of this, I suddenly "blew up" at something she did, something she knew was not permitted. Just as sudden as my explosion was a look of peace which returned to her young face. With a shock I realized that by changing my usual standards, I had only compounded the confusion she felt at our move. Not only did people speak words she could not understand, not only were her meals different and her bedroom gone, she now seemed to have a mother who no longer cared about the things she had once said were important.

Two years later, at five, this same daughter was playing with friends in the garden of our Vienna house. We were glad that her German had advanced enough so that she could have playmates, and happy that two Viennese children had come. Suddenly Susan ran into the house frightened and indignant. "Am I an American?" she asked. "Of course," we assured her, "Everyone in our family is American, but we are living in Austria for a few years." "Hannse said I'm not American. I can't be." "Why ever not?" "Because I don't know anything about playing cowboys. I've never even ridden a horse."

That fall when we returned to the States, Susan was with us on a ride through New England's countryside. When we stopped at a farm stand to buy some apples, Susan asked to get them. She walked a few steps toward the farmer, then returned to ask, "What language will he speak?" A roadside stand in Austria meant German. What did it mean here?

After this New England visit to my father, we moved back to the Washington home we had left two years earlier. Dickie, now three, lacked the homecoming enthusiasm the rest of us shared. When we showed friends home movies of our life in Austria we learned why. As soon as the Vienna house flashed on the screen, our three-year-old sat up straight on the couch, pointed to the movie and proclaimed happily, "There's Dickie's house." Sitting in the living room he had come to as a new born baby and had left ten months later, he recognized his home in the films of Austria. It made me wonder what "home" meant to these multi-homed children. Sometimes they wondered, too.

En route to New Zealand, we stopped a day for sightseeing in San Francisco. The Bay Harbor cruise looked inviting, and our three children quickly made friends with other youngsters on board. As the adults listened to the guide, the children played games around the benches on the boat. Our youngest was in serious conversation with another little girl. They asked and answered each other's questions until I noticed our daughter seemed perplexed. She came across the aisle, and put her head on my lap. "Mom, Jane lives in New York," she said and asked the question that has echoed through years of transfers: "Mom, where do I live?" The answer has always been the same, "Wherever *we* are."

Did the changing homes, the changing languages, the sometimes-changing mother make life over-difficult for our children? When they were grown, I asked each one separately, "What was the hardest thing about Foreign Service life for you?" All three answers, each given instantly, were identical, "Always being different."

When they were in Washington they were different because they didn't know the latest movies or songs or styles. They couldn't talk about "last summer in Vienna" without sounding as if they were showing off. Susan had a junior high classmate who was moving to Chicago. Her class was in seventh grade hysterics over the pending departure. "We'll never see you again," they moaned. "People you never see again live in Austria or New Zealand," said my daughter, "they do not just move to Chicago."

Overseas, our children were different because they were Americans in another land. In Austria Barbara wore shorts in a public park and was laughed at, "Only boys wear shorts." The shorts went home to a Stateside cousin. In New Zealand she had a Christmas party dress, a new black velveteen jumper with fancy white blouse with red roses on its collar. She was laughed at again. "No one wears black to a party." The dress went home, too. Soon her saddle shoes followed.

I hadn't realized about the saddle shoes until that day at the town library in Lower Hutt, New Zealand. Wherever we lived we sought out the local library and its children's section to borrow books. I was enjoying the bright sun-filled room and feeling quite at peace. What fun it was to be in an English speaking country where we would have a multitude of books to choose from. Barbara was looking through the children's bookshelves when I saw her move quickly to a library table and stand with her feet carefully underneath it. Three little girls from her kindergarten had just entered the room. They waved pleasantly to my newcomer, and she waved back, but kept her rigid stance at the table. Only after her classmates had left would she move, and she said quickly, "Let's go home now." The explanation came somewhat later. The two feet hastily hidden under the library table had been wearing American saddle shoes; all six New Zealand kindergarten feet had worn their typical black oxfords. What a dreadful burden to bear at five—to talk differently, to wear the wrong dresses, and to have the only saddle shoes in the country.

For our son, the clothing problem was a little different. En route to New Zealand, we had told him that most of the boys there wore short pants. "Well, I won't," firmly answered this third grader in his full-length gray pants. One visit to his prospective school, and we were at the shop in Wellington buying a gray shirt, a school sweater, school cap, school tie and short gray pants.

It was easy to modify clothing for the children, but there were many things we could not change. Frequent uprooting, adjusting to new homes and customs, leaving friends both here and abroad were constant challenges in their lives. I once saw a family in the international departure lounge at the Baltimore airport waiting to board their overseas plane. In each of four phone booths sat one of their children making a last farewell call to a friend. Immediately I knew this was a family being transferred abroad, the parents perhaps willingly, the younger members reluctantly.

There were benefits, too, for our traveling children. I was comforted when, after the first day in his new Maryland fifth grade, our son walked into the kitchen and announced, "Well, I don't have a friend yet, but I know I will." That knowledge was a gift of his experiences in finding his way in a succession of new groups. Other gifts were a world awareness. Anything about posts where we have lived or where friends have lived carries a special meaning for each of us.

Perhaps the most important gift was the family closeness we might or might not have had in another career. Each time we moved, our children had only each other as friends. With our sequence of girl, boy, girl, each a few years apart in age, when we were living in the States, they went their separate ways. In transit or at a new post, they were forced to rediscover each other and they became very close. They knew their father and I were in another country to serve the United States, and we always felt they were proud of our work.

Proud, yes, but none of them chose to follow our footsteps. Perhaps it was because their father and I were so obviously happy each time we returned home. Perhaps they were tired of being different, even if diplomatic difference meant being special. They all chose careers of service: family counselor, geriatric nurse, government economist. None of their careers requires moving.

Surgeries Abroad

"International Medical Consultant; Pediatrics a specialty." I have not seen the job description in a newspaper, but I know I have the qualifications.

For almost thirty years we were a Foreign Service family moving around the globe. Our children have been in hospitals in New Zealand, Austria, Germany. Pediatricians in those countries remain on our Christmas card list today.

The first hospitalization was in 1954 in Austria. I had gone upstairs in our Vienna home to waken our two-year-old from his nap and found him propped up on one elbow, trembling violently. When I picked him up I felt his great heat, and when I spoke to him softly, his eyes rolled back. It was the first fever convulsion I had ever seen. I knew we needed a doctor right away.

In occupied Vienna of post World War II, we had two sources of medical help: the U.S. military hospital established for the GI's stationed in Austria as part of the four-country occupation forces; or Dr. H., an Austrian pediatrician we had come to know well. And he made house calls.

On this day my mind darted back and forth. Should I call Dr. H. with whom I spoke only German? Would my German suffice? Or should I take the baby to the Army hospital where my language would serve, but the doctor on duty would probably not be a pediatrician. Need for communication won. My husband, still in a thigh high cast from a broken leg, swung himself into the back seat of our car. I put Dickie on his lap and drove the three miles to the hospital. Pulling up at the gate, I left Fred in the back seat, grabbed our son and pushed past the startled guard on duty, "I don't have time to get out my passport, but I'm an American and my baby is very sick." Inside we were immediately directed to a doctor. With my head full of the turmoil of choosing which doctor, I looked at the medic in his U.S. Army uniform and asked, "Do you speak English?" He did, and he was able to help Dickie. He didn't comment on the rattled mother.

Six months later we returned to the same hospital. Dickie's four-year-old sister was to have a tonsillectomy. This time the choice was between hospitals, not doctors. It was not a difficult decision. Vienna's once famous clinics were in bad decline, old, out of date, and not clean. I could not have put a child in them. At the military hospital, I planned to stay with Susan until she was sedated, but a stern army officer forbade it. He insisted I wait in the hospital bedroom as they wheeled the child away for surgery. Susan did not appear frightened then, but for several weeks afterwards she asked me to "promise" to stay at home during her naps. Since we had household help at the time, I usually did any errands while the children slept, so that I could be with them when they were awake. In deference to Susan's wishes, I changed my routine and stayed home during her afternoon naps. This lasted several weeks until she was, I assumed, no longer afraid of what might happen if she fell asleep during the daytime.

Our second tonsillectomy was four years later back in Washington. Children's Hospital was quite willing to let me stay with Dickie until he was asleep. The scary part in this surgery came, not from the hospital but from me—when we brought the patient home. His first snack was the traditional ice cream followed by Jell-O. Soon afterwards he asked for toast. I carried two pieces to the couch where he rested, and then, returning to the kitchen, I panicked. I had just sent dry toast down a seven-year-old's raw throat. I could feel the pain in my own neck. What kind of a mother was I? I made myself go back to the living room where he was smiling and comfortably sucking the toast, but I remember the panic.

We used to joke that our three children thought that if they all had their surgeries in the same country, their parents might find it boring.

In 1961 Barbara chose New Zealand as the place to dispense with her tonsils. Not even the U.S. Army could have kept me from being with her, and not just because of Susan's experience. At five, Barbara had had all the shocks she could manage for one year. She had left her home and friends in the States, had moved into and out of two homes in New Zealand, had been laughed at for being "different" and for "talking funny." She had been in the car with me the day we returned from nursery school to find our first New Zealand home on fire. I did not think she needed to be alone in the hospital.

"In the United States, we always stay with a child," I exaggerated to the Wellington hospital where parents "never do."

"I must stay," I asserted to the reluctant surgeon who objected: "Mrs. Irving, if you see blood when she comes back to her room, you'll get upset and upset the child."

His final argument gave me pause: "All right, Mrs. Irving," he conceded, "but if she hemorrhages, it will be your fault and not mine."

The warning shook me until Fred reminded me I was not apt to get hysterical over blood, and that if Barbara started to hemorrhage, mine would be the most calming face she could see. I stayed. The hospital staff, obviously confused by my presence, gave me the other bed in Barbara's room and gave me a patient menu to check for my meal choices.

Soon the hospital came to know me. Within the year our two older children had their appendixes out there: one, an emergency; one, scheduled after months of chronic pain. Although I did not stay overnight with these older two, the hospital was surprised that I stayed during the day. Before each surgery the doctor assured me he would phone me at home as soon as the operation was over.

"Oh, I'll be there. Doesn't the hospital have a waiting room?" It did, a tiny room with four bulky chairs and a window facing the street. I felt it was not often used. I brought my own book.

When the children had recovered, the surgeon asked if I wouldn't like to volunteer at the hospital. He had noticed how much time I had been able to spend there, he said. Somehow, I was not able to make clear that it wasn't for lack of things to do that I sat there those many hours.

After the New Zealand operations, our surgeries were complete, but the pattern of three countries was repeated when our children had their teeth straightened.

Susan had hers done in New Zealand by the "best man in the field." He said her mouth was overcrowded, and he would remove some teeth to make more space. An upper and a lower tooth were removed on one side only, leaving Susan with an uncrowded, straight row of teeth—slightly off center. In her forties, she was back in orthodontia.

Rick's orthodontia was done in Washington. To this waiting room mother, the many visits seemed endless and the book I was reading, appropriate for the occasion. The report of the Kennedy presidency, it was titled, *A Thousand Days.*

Barbara combined two—really three—countries in her task. She began with Rick's orthodontist in Washington, but our family was transferred to Vienna before the job was completed.

"Fortunately," said our Washington specialist, "there is a young man at the army hospital in Munich who has been trained in this technique. Contact him."

"Just think," said a friend, "how reasonable it will be. Military hospitals charge only two dollars a visit." It was less of a bargain when one added round trip airfares from Vienna to Munich for Barbara and an accompanying parent. On one visit the army dentist told us he would be in Vienna the following month and would willingly bring his tools to our home to check her braces there. Barbara sat in an armchair in the upstairs bathroom facing a bright sunny window while the orthodontist adjusted her braces. It was the only dental house call our family ever had.

Normal childhood illnesses spread across the globe without favoritism. Stomach infections in Jamaica, fever convulsions in Austria and Washington, measles in New Zealand—a severe case while I was out of town making a speech on "Family Life in America" (something seemed twisted here, I thought); undiagnosed whooping cough on the ocean trip home from our first tour in Austria; colds, cuts, flus, insect bites everywhere.

When we lived in Iceland, I was invited to address the monthly meeting of the U.S.-Icelandic nurses group. I was asked because I was the wife of the U.S. Ambassador, not because of my medical knowledge. Still, as I told them, I did feel qualified to speak on illnesses in many lands.

It is because of these qualifications that I now offer my services.

If you plan a tonsillectomy in Austria, an appendectomy in New Zealand, bring your questions to me. If you are overseas and considering surgery, orthodontia or measles, feel free to call.

Calm at Five

(Life at home in Arlington. A tale in words of one syllable)

When our three kids were young, we had a rule in our house: each day from five to six, you may not fight. When the clock says five, an old fight must stop. When it reads five, new fights may not start. You may not tease or push or pout. You may not fight.

Our three kids knew the rule. Their friends knew it too. Ann stopped by with Sue on their way home from third grade.
"Is it true?" she asked, "that you can't fight for an hour?"
"That's right," said Sue. "She means it."
John came by to pick up Rick, and he was told the rule.
"What's with your Mom?" (I was glad I knew John liked me. I liked him, too.) "What's up, Rick?"
"Don't ask me. Ask her," shrugged Rick, and away the two went on their bikes.

Our friends soon heard of the rule.
"Is what we heard true? You don't let them fight from five to six?"
"Yep, it's a house rule. It's a good one."
"Oh," said George. He made the "oh" have two sounds that went up at the end.
"Why don't you just let them?" asked Jane. "What's the sense? All kids fight with their sibs."
"Of course. I know they do, and I know mine do, too, but they may not do it from five to six. Five is the time of day they are most tired. I'm tired then, too. A frown one would skip at noon will cause a

fight at five. A nit no one would pick at two is a cause to fight at five. That's how life is. The rule makes sense to me."

And why did it end at six? Near six we ate, and once they were full of food they were more apt to take the chips off their shirt sleeves and be friends. Then, too, once they ate, it was too near bed time to fight. A fight then could mean time for bed if the clock said so or not.

Our friends knew I was a kind Mom and that I loved my kids. They knew I would be up all night with a sick child and not say one cross word. Our three kids knew this too. They knew they could count on me to help them when they had need of help. And they knew they had a strange Mom who had this strange rule. But, then, most kids think their Moms and Dads have odd minds that do not work the same way a kid's does.

I know the rule did not hurt them at all. I think it may have helped keep peace when they were tired. We're glad to say the three of them still like us and we like them. "You may not fight from five to six" is now part of our home's lore. And, now and then, an old friend from their school days will say to one of our three,

"Say, your Mom was the one who had that strange rule. Tell me, did she let you fight all the rest of the day?"

RETURN TO VIENNA 1967-68

A Challenging year

Life at Linneplatz

The house on Linneplatz went with the job—Deputy Chief of Mission at the American Embassy in Vienna. During our first tour in Austria many years earlier, we had attended functions there, always arriving early and waiting outside in our car until the proper moment for a junior officer to enter. Now, in August of 1967, we and our three children were moving in to make it our home.

The house was said to have been a king's summer palace, and its appearance made it easy to believe such an origin. It stood in a row of large stone homes facing a small city park. French doors in the living room and the dining room opened onto a stone verandah that looked like the setting from an opera; its curved cement railing topped by urns of flowers overlooked the city-sized walled garden below. Had anyone in my family had a singing voice, we might have tried an aria standing there, at its conclusion descending the broad curved staircase to the garden paths.

Inside, the elegant dining room also spoke of operas and kings. At one end a large gold-framed mirror hung over a richly carved buffet. A tapestry hunting scene covered the adjacent wall. Gold and white dining room chairs were upholstered in dark red velvet. The long polished table, lovely at formal dinners for twenty-two, looked overwhelming at our family breakfasts for four.

That first day, as we opened the gate, I remembered fifteen years earlier handing my calling cards through it into the garden-muddied hands of the little boy whose family then lived there.

We mounted the home's stone steps to enter the tall arched front door. Inside, a reception room was furnished with small tables, chairs, and a couch under the window. To brighten this dark room, I always kept a bowl of fresh flowers on the far table. Whenever the Ambassador or his wife was expected at a function, our children would kneel on the couch to watch out the window for the official car. It is a Foreign Service courtesy to greet an Ambassador at the door. With this couple it was not only a courtesy; it was a requirement. As soon as our son or daughter sighted the black limousine flying an American flag, they came rushing to summon us from our other guests. "They're here," and we were waiting at the door by the time the car pulled up.

We called this first room St. Anne's Hall, named for the almost life sized wooden statue that stood on the left as we entered. Whether it was she or not, I never knew, nor even why we so named her, but to us she was St. Anne. We came to greet her warmly on any return after a trip, "We're back, St. Anne," or to ask for luck on an important departure, "Wish us well." When, after three weeks in the house, Susan left to start college in the States, we saluted St. Anne as we left for the airport for that first break in our family.

St. Anne's Hall opened to two large connecting living rooms. The farther one held a stone fireplace and opened onto that operatic verandah. In the nearer room stood the baby grand piano, and from it I learned a little more about how deeply music permeated the life of the Viennese. While playing an opera melody one day, I heard voices and realized that the cook in the kitchen and the gardener under the window were both singing the complete words of the aria.

This room also held the couch where Susan slept several nights before her college departure. The house was being painted when we moved in, and her room was not finished. Painting in Vienna was an undertaking that required removing all the interior doors for refinishing and thus removing all privacy. On painting days we had to be up, showered and dressed before the 7:00 AM arrival of those conscientious workmen.

Behind the first living room a door led to the home's beautiful staircase. Wide enough for four people, with polished wood railing, deep red carpeting held in place by shining brass rods, the stairway led up to a floor-to-ceiling window on the landing, and then turned back on itself to complete the climb to the second floor.

There it opened into a large square center hall with rooms on either side. On one side was the master suite: bedroom, bath, and study, all with broad windows overlooking the garden. In this bedroom we received a 4:00 AM telephone call from Susan the night of Martin

Luther King's murder. She called from her Washington vacation to tell us about the murder and to say that parts of Washington were in flames. After we had talked for some time, she suddenly asked, "I hope I didn't wake you up. What time is it there?" I replied that it was four in the morning, but that we really appreciated her phone call. It is a gift for any parent if a college age child wishes to touch base with you when there is a crisis.

Here, too, in this bedroom we kept the cardboard sign we had made. Because my husband and I differed with the Ambassador and his wife on many values, we knew that at any time one of us might "blow it" and be asked to leave. An Ambassador has this authority. Some issues were too important to us to hedge on or to overlook, issues such as comments on how one viewed people of color, for example. We trod a narrow line in our relations with this top family, and had made the "start packing" sign to post when needed. Although we were never asked to leave, more than once each of us arrived home to find the other had taped the sign on the bedroom door.

To the right of the bedroom was the master bath, a large room with all the usual equipment plus a long padded table, presumably for massages. (We kept our extra towels there.) I recall standing by that table in a white evening dress holding cold compresses to Barbara's bleeding nose. I would not leave the house until she was all right. I knew we were then ten minutes late for the pre-dinner hour at the Ambassador's Residence, something that was never done, as my hostess told me firmly on our belated arrival. But, I knew, also, that, were I in Rome when Rome was collapsing, and my daughter was bleeding, my responsibility would be to my daughter, not to Rome. Perhaps it was time for the sign to go up.

To the left of the bedroom was the study where my husband and I each had our desks. This became our family room in preference to the more formal rooms downstairs. When Fred and I were going out for the evening, Rick and Barbara had their supper in this study. Their eating time was our dressing time, so we could chat and be together for a while. Ever since the evening in New Zealand, some years earlier, when one of our three had gone into guffaws of laughter at the first sight of her father in top hat and tails, we could never become too impressed with how wonderful we were sure we looked, not even when

I wore a ball gown and my long white kid gloves.

On my desk in the study were two phones, one for general outside use and one an extension of the Embassy switchboard. When the Embassy line rang, it was either my husband or the Ambassador's wife. When it was not my husband, I stood up to talk. The Ambassador's wife had very strong ideas and wishes and I could not have sat casually while speaking with her, even on the phone. From this desk I arranged housing, food and medical support for American students being evacuated from Czechoslovakia when the Soviets invaded Prague the summer of 1968. My husband worked with both governments to ensure safe passage for the students across the border into Vienna. I was responsible for caring for them once they arrived. I arranged for cots and bedding to be set up in the high school gym, a roster of parents to be on duty all night, a doctor on call, ready to come to the train station or the high school. After working around the clock for thirty-six hours, Fred and I went down to the station to meet the sealed train as it came in. I have a vivid memory of one cheery student saying thanks, she was glad to be safely out, and she would call her Stateside parents in a few days to say she was fine. I led her to the phone bank we had arranged and urged her, "Call them today." The world had been watching the Prague invasion, and there were many worried parents who should not have to wait a "few days" to learn their child was safe. After all the students were safely housed, Fred and I returned home at 8:30 AM. Before falling into bed, I phoned each wife who had volunteered to help. And, standing, I phoned to report to the Ambassador's wife.

Across from our suite on the second floor were two more bedrooms. Barbara's was pretty with old-fashioned furniture and a small stone balcony over the front door facing the park. It seemed just right for an almost teenage girl. Next to it, Rick's was the same size with heavier furniture and a window seat instead of a balcony. I'm sure that if I saw that window seat today, emanating from it would still be the strains of "The House of the Rising Sun," our son's favorite record, soon everyone else's least favorite. I accused him of ignoring the beauties of Vienna and spending his first six months sitting on the windowsill gazing west—towards home—while that record played constantly. At the end of his school year, we promised him a trip home to stay with friends for two weeks. When he left Austria carrying a Viennese street sign as a gift to his best friend, he promised to send a wire as soon as he reached Washington. Addressed to my husband and me the wire contained two words: "Thanks, Rick."

The children's rooms shared a bath to the side and the home's large storage closet. When we moved in I recognized the names scotch taped on the shelves of that closet. Six years earlier, good Foreign Service friends had preceded us in the job and the house, and it was the names of their five children I read. It pleased me to see them there, and the nametags stayed as long as we did. We just taped the names of our three children next to their five.

Before Susan returned at Christmas, her third floor bedroom was finished, painted her chosen light green. Its bookshelves held her favorite books and her still beloved Little Women dolls. Finally, she had a bed and a room of her own. Her view faced the home's garden and the city beyond. On New Year's Eve, we all watched the lights of Vienna from her top balcony, and then Susan, my husband and I put on formal clothes and went to attend the Viennese tradition of a gala New Year's opera. During intermission we, like the rest of the audience, went into the lobby of that ornate opera house and strolled—people watching of the nth degree. After one false start on our part, we strolled counterclockwise like the rest of the opera-goers.

In two years we left Linneplatz to return to Washington where my husband had been asked to take on a new job. We bade St. Anne farewell for the last time.

Rank Has its Privileges—Junior Style

The second time we lived in Vienna, our son, Rick, began to hide his shoes. He said he had to. It was the only way he could keep them from receiving a daily polish. Please understand, he was a teen-aged American boy, and mirror-like shoes were not part of his persona, not even during these two years he was living in Vienna, that city where rank and appearance were so important; that city where street laborers commonly carried their sandwich lunches in briefcases; where the drug store delivery driver wore a white lab coat to confirm his membership in the medical profession; Vienna, where every adult male wore shoes regularly polished to a fresh gloss.

Our family was in Austria for two years during our second tour at the Embassy there. It was the woman who helped us in our home who was determined to polish Rick's shoes.

"Mom, can't you make her understand?" he pled.

We tried to explain to Maria that Rick didn't want his shoes polished.

"He is the son of the house. They must be."

We tried to explain that if he wanted them polished, he would do it himself.

"The son of such high ranking people must not shine his own shoes."

We tried to explain that in America, all boys do such things for themselves.

Silence.

So, every day after school, Rick hid his shoes.

It was not the first time he had faced the problem of rank in Austria. All over the world, U.S. Embassy buildings are guarded by a select group of Marines. In Vienna, our contingent of twenty-six had a house not far from our own in the 17th district. A particularly nice group of young men, they acted as big brothers to all the Embassy children, and Rick frequently stopped by Marine House after school. One day, as he was leaving, one of the Marines offered him a box of leftover electrical odds and ends, items dear to the heart of a teen-age boy. Rick walked home, large carton under his arm, and started up the front stairs of our house.

"Stop," said the painters working in the front hall. They eyed the cardboard carton and assumed he was a workman. "You have to go around to the side door."

Rick, assuming the front hall was full of ladders or the paint still wet, willingly went to the side door.

"Stop," said the cook at the side door. "You must not come in this way. You are the son of the house. Use the front door."

As Rick told it later, he really didn't care which door he came in, but he hoped to get in his own house somehow.

Some years earlier Rick's older sister had been offered special treatment in this formal city. During our first tour in Vienna, we were visiting the home of American friends. As we got ready to leave, their Austrian maid helped the adults into coats. I looked around and saw my three-year-old standing still, her arms outstretched, waiting to have her coat put on by this helper. I could see the child was only copying the adults, but you may well believe I interceded.

"Thank you, but Susan is very proud that she can now put on her own coat," I said firmly.

Two years later, five-year-old Susan went into our neighborhood bakery to pick up some fresh bread while I waited in the car. I noticed that she was served immediately while Viennese customers were still waiting in line. I quickly went into the shop. I thanked the proprietress for trying to make my children feel welcome and at home by helping them right away, but in their own country, they would wait in line and I wished them to do so here. The bakeshop lady smiled at me, and we had a friendly understanding thereafter.

Foreign Service friends who had lived in the Far East told me that the problem of special treatment was even more difficult to overcome there; most homes had several household helpers. As one mother put it. "I don't want my kids to forget how to pick up their own pajamas. Who will be doing it when we go home?"

It was not the pajamas I worried about. I was sure my maternal dominance would be strong enough to insist that clothes be picked up wherever we lived. But I did have concern lest my Foreign Service children grow up with any sense of entitlement or expectation of special treatment. Overseas we lived in larger houses than we had at home. We often had household helpers, and there was this prevalent attitude of "rank." Our children knew that some privileges came to their father and me as senior Embassy members, and that many responsibilities came our way, also. Only a little of this touched them directly—most often the responsibility of being a representative American. As I so often reminded, "You may be the only American that shopkeeper ever meets." The privilege side of our jobs seemed to have no role in their lives or in their thinking. Our first summer in Iceland, I stopped worrying about its effect on them.

That year, Susan was working in Boston, and Rick and his younger sister, Barbara, looked for jobs in Iceland. Of the openings they found—at the hotel desk in Reykjavík, the summer theater there, and a fish packing plant—they chose the packing plant.

"It's the most Icelandic," they said.

Early each morning, they went off to work in their high rubber boots—Rick, to stand in the cold room where the trucks dumped their tons of fish on the floor, and his crew shoveled it onto a conveyor belt; Barbara, at the cutting tables, where, in groups of four, girls sliced, cut and cleaned the fish over tables lit from below. Each evening when Rick and Barbara came home from work it was now their parents, not a painter, who insisted they use the back door. The odor of fish preceded them and told us they were home. Even in Iceland, where the smell of fish is called the smell of money, the city runs special buses for the aromatic freezing plant employees.

It was Barbara's accident that summer at the freezing plant that put my mind at ease and convinced me that exposure to diplomatic life had not destroyed our children's American values.

I returned home one afternoon to find her resting on the den couch. She looked pale, and I asked, "Was it a hard day? You look really tired." She held up a finger wrapped in layers of bandage. It had been cut that morning at work. The people from the plant had taken her to the doctor, who stitched it up and bandaged it. Then Barbara had assured them she could return to finish her day at work, which she did. At the hospital, she had given her name and her street address, 23 Laufasvegur. She had not said the American Embassy; she had not said her father was the American Ambassador. After I got over my concern at not being there when she was hurt, I was very proud of her. Not only had she handled it well alone at seventeen, she had done it without falling back on use of "rank."

Some years later, in Jamaica, a newspaper article about me ended with the sentence, "Mrs. Irving has three grown children." Barbara commented, "It should have added, 'All of whom turned out well.'" "So far," I replied.

We are now retired and I remain proud of them all. Sue can still put on her own coat; Barbara still handles crises well; Rick comes in any door he wishes. His shoes don't shine.

Those Who Drove

The first time we were senior enough to merit an official driver was in 1967 when my husband became Deputy Ambassador to Austria. Herr Goetz, the man who held the job, was a good and kind man. He was Santa Claus at Embassy Christmas parties and much loved by all the Embassy children, both those who recognized the man in the red suit and those who did not. Herr Goetz spoke little English, our German was only fair, but every day we talked to each other. As my husband would munch a crisp Viennese roll en route to yet another cocktail party, meanwhile groaning at the demands of Vienna's constant social life, Herr Goetz would say sympathetically, "*Ach, Das leben von einem diplomat.*" Ah, the life of a diplomat. He knew how often we would rather be at home. When he drove me somewhere during the day he would explain buildings, areas of the city, and sometimes the politics of Vienna. He always ended with "*Wissen Sie, Madam?*" Do you know, Madam? To write the German words is to hear him say them.

In Vienna that fall, the first official event I attended alone was held on a rainy fall afternoon at the Pallavacini Palace, a large ornate building in the old gray inner city. Everyone at the women's reception was beautifully dressed. The uniformed waiters, the Viennese orchestra, the rich food, and the ornately decorated room seemed to epitomize a courtly Europe of old. I was delighted that I would not have to drive myself home from such a glamorous event. When I came out of the palace into the five-thirty darkness, I saw Herr Goetz double-parked directly in front of the door. Other guests, seeking their drivers, looked up and down the street in the rain. As I walked down the palace steps, Herr Goetz saw me, stepped out of the car and opened the door. It was always thus with him. We arrived on time, and he was there when it was time to leave.

Only once did I think he would make us late for our destination: the day we made our final departure from Vienna. He drove our family the twenty-five miles to Schwechat Airport at a speed that felt like ten miles an hour. The drive was uncharacteristically silent; I heard no, "Wissen Sie, Madam?" When we arrived at the airport, his wife was already there. She had taken the bus all that distance to tell us goodbye. She stood next to her husband as they watched us walk across the tarmac to board our plane. As long as the Goetz's lived, our families exchanged Christmas cards. On my bureau I have the china swan they gave us the night we had coffee at their apartment.

The two drivers we had when Fred was an Ambassador also became special people to our family.

First there was Ottó in Iceland, who would gladly have bent any rule for us.

"We can park here" (This in a no parking zone). "The Ambassador's car doesn't have to obey the rules."

Our response: "The Ambassador's car will always obey the rules."

"If I blur the date on Barbara's driver's application we can get her a license." (Our then sixteen-year-old daughter was disappointed that she did not meet Iceland's age requirement of eighteen.)

"No blurring of dates."

"You don't need stamps. The Ambassador's wife can send her mail through the Embassy."

"That's for official mail."

"Anything the Ambassador's wife writes is official."

"My notes are personal. They need stamps."

Soon he learned the kind of people we were, and soon we learned how much he wanted to help us, that he would always be there when we needed him. When he was driving us somewhere, the slightest mention from us of the people we were about to visit, would bring forth helpful information about the family. Each time we returned from a business trip to Washington, Ottó used the forty-five minute drive from the airport to fill us in on politics, personalities, and changes during our absence.

He made many trips to the airport for many reasons. On one memorable morning he took us there in a snowstorm so bad that he drove with his head out the car window to see the road. Our younger daughter was departing for Christmas in Austria, and, although Ottó disapproved of her leaving home for Christmas, he was determined to get her to the plane on time. When we reached the airport his head was covered in snow and frost. The desk clerk who knew him (as did everyone in Iceland) handed him a large white towel to dry off.

Ottó's fastest trip to the airport came during President Nixon's visit to Iceland. While the President was in the country, Air Force One remained at Keflavík Airport. My husband, our daughter, and I were invited to visit the plane to see the presidential quarters. Ottó looked forward to this opportunity even more than did we. Because of a delayed start from Reykjavík, it seemed we might not reach the airport at the appointed hour, but Ottó broke all speed limits to get there. My husband said not a word. I noticed that Ottó left the plane with several Air Force One matchbooks.

The only problem this driver had with us arose whenever we attended an event at the Soviet Embassy. He refused to park the official American car in front of their building. Ottó's father had been a leader in the Danish Resistance during World War II, and this son reacted strongly to any country he felt threatened freedom or democracy. He would deliver us to the front door and then park the car a block up the hill, watching closely enough to see us when we came out.

In addition to the regular rounds of diplomatic stops, Ottó drove me to the hospital where I worked with the Red Cross, to the girls' high school to make a speech, and to the school for deaf children. One day I visited a woman I had met when her daughter and our daughter worked together in the local fish factory. The family's home, nestled deep in a lava field outside of Reykjavík, was barely visible from the main road; the car could go only part way. That day Ottó declared that with us he went places in Iceland even he had never been before.

At our next post, Jamaica, our official driver, Mr. Hudson, was a skilled driver, a friendly and knowledgeable man. Trained in police work and protection, Mr. Hudson made sure we were safe everywhere we went. He drove me to schools all over Jamaica: the Rastafarian center in the hills of Kingston, the all-age school in the far west at Savannah la Mar, the country summer camp for underprivileged children, the

School on Jamaica House grounds, the primary school in the violence rife slums of Kingston. In that era of unpredictable violence, the Embassy felt better if I had the protection of Mr. Hudson's presence. A further benefit, I knew, was his warmth and friendliness to those we visited. When I came out of a school at the end of a morning I would find him showing an interested group of children how the automatic windows on the car worked, or talking with them about the Americans he knew. I told him he was as good a spokesperson for the United States as I tried to be.

In the 1960s and 1970s an Ambassador's wife could use the official car if it was for official business or for the benefit of the Embassy, as determined by the Ambassador. In later years, some abuse of this privilege (being driven to hairdressing appointments, etc.) combined with a penny-counting Congress to result in denying an Ambassador's wife any use of the car. I think the complete restriction was a mistake. When I arrived anywhere in the Embassy car, people knew it was the Ambassador's wife and it gave prestige to the visit. It was a way of demonstrating American interest in this school, this hospital, this library, this remote section of the country. When I worked in areas that might be dangerous, it made sense to have a driver trained in security measures.

When my husband was going into an area prone to violence, he was the one who used the official car. One day a prominent Jamaican politician needed to go into a zone of Kingston filled with his political opponents, an area known to have a lot of violence. He phoned and asked if my husband would accompany him. "I know I'll be safe if I'm with the American Ambassador," the politician said. My husband made sure Mr. Hudson was his driver on that trip. Some in the Embassy looked down on the drivers, but I told him, "Just remember, Mr. Hudson," I said, "No one in the Embassy can say their job is more important than yours. When you drive, you have the Ambassador's life in your hands."

Once Mr. Hudson showed concern about my safety. I had been invited to visit a home in the countryside a few miles from Kingston. The only way to reach it was to leave the highway and walk up over a shrub covered hill to the house. When I convinced Mr. Hudson that I knew the family and I would be safe, he drove me and the daughter of the house to a point she indicated on the main road. Then she and I climbed the path up through the brush to her parents' home. When we reappeared two hours later, Mr. Hudson was at the roadside. He seemed relieved to see us. Like Ottó, Mr. Hudson would say that with our family he went places he had never been before.

One evening we gave Mr. Hudson a different assignment. In the midst of preparation for a large dinner party at the Residence, we heard radio reports of riots in downtown Kingston. Our cook was worried about her two children who were in the vicinity of the riot area. There was no way to telephone to see if they were all right. "I'll ask Mr. Hudson to take you down," I said. "If everything is all right come back to help us. Bring the children along if you will feel better."

"I can't go so close to your dinner," she answered.

"If it were my children I would need to know they were safe. If you can't come back, we'll manage." She went, found the children safe with a relative, and returned to finish preparations for dinner before our guests arrived.

It was a sad trip when Mr. Hudson drove us to the Kingston airport for the last time. I can still see him sitting on the bench outside the terminal on that warm November day in his dark pants, dark tie, white shirt, looking sad. We were sad, too. He had been our good friend.

When I think of Herr Goetz, Ottó, Mr. Hudson, I know that having a driver is what I miss most from Foreign Service life. What I particularly miss is the good men who were in the jobs when we lived in their countries. They served well. As employees of the Embassy, they served the United States. By constantly helping us better understand their countries they served their own homelands, also. We thank them.

ALONG THE WAY

The Parents

Heart Attack

In February of 1969, four months after we returned from Vienna, I had a heart attack. When it happened, I didn't know what it was. I only knew I had to sit down "right away." In the center of my chest was a large block of cement that felt about 2 by 4 by 8 inches. Behind it was a glowing circle of flame. The cement was very heavy, warm and soft. I knew that if it hardened it would be too late. I didn't think too late for what.

"I don't feel well." I put down the spatula from the breakfast egg I was frying. "I think I have to sit down. Right now." With one glance, my husband was at my side, helping me to the den couch. My hairline was wet with perspiration. My arms were heavy and numb. "I'll phone the doctor," Fred had once seen a heart attack and suspected what my gray lips meant. He left our junior high daughter by my side. "The ambulance is on the way," he returned. "Barbara, watch at the door."

"I can't breathe. There's no air in here. Open the window." Fred looked at the open window. "Sure," he said. The lump in my chest was getting heavier. I wanted to cry but didn't seem to have the energy for tears.

In minutes hurrying feet brought the EMTs, medical bags in hand. Minutes more and I was on the stretcher in the ambulance and soon at Suburban Hospital. Our family doctor met us in the emergency room. I know he wore a nice tweed jacket, for I was sorry to be sick on the sleeve of it. The rest of the morning is a haze. Some exams, I think, and then being put in the Intensive Care Cardiac unit. My desperate desire for sleep overcame me. And I felt filled with gratitude for the monitors someone attached to my chest. I would not need to say what was happening to me or to judge what should be attended to. All anxiety over decisions was gone. I need do nothing but sleep.

Fred was allowed to see me five minutes every second hour, and spent three days on the bench outside the cardiac unit—on call for any change in my condition and ready for his allotted short visits. One visit was given to daughter Susan who had flown home from college. "Why isn't she at school?" I thought. By the third day I still wanted only sleep, sleep, sleep, but I was able to be moved from the glass-walled intensive care unit to a room on the cardiac floor. I knew I was healing a little for I was alert enough to be further intrigued by the monitoring devices, those specially designed pads and tapes, and to think how many American industries must be making tiny devices that have one use only—a whole field of inventions of which I was unaware, and inventors somewhere whom I should thank.

In the hospital room our doctor expressed the hope that perhaps it had been something other than a heart attack; a final test would show. I realized how much I hoped this would be so when it wasn't. Damaged heart muscle in the blood established that it had been a real heart attack. Tears I had been too weak to shed at home came gushing out. Dr. K. gave me Kleenex and sympathy. I couldn't even think what this meant for my future life, and only wanted to see my husband, who arrived a few minutes later to a crying wife needing his shoulder. He sat by my bed hugging me as I wept out the sad news.

In 1969, a heart attack meant a three-week hospital stay. During those weeks, I realized how grateful I was for the timing of the attack. The Saturday morning I had it—the exact day between Valentine's Day and Heart Sunday—was also the day of our son's College Board exams. I was glad he had left for school before I became sick. When he came home at noon, he saw an open carton of eggs on the counter across from the kitchen door, and sensed the emptiness of the house. A neighbor arrived quickly to tell him we had gone to Suburban Hospital, and he drove there to join us.

For all of us, at last, the three-week hospitalization ended, and I came home to more care and rest. An intercom from bedroom to kitchen helped my family know what I wanted for supper—until the neighbors next door commented they were glad I was well enough to try roast chicken now. The emotional recovery was the hardest part, the slow return of enough nervous energy to drive or to "do battle." On my first department store shopping trip, a clerk in the sweater department was rushed and rude. Too emotionally weak to argue or demand, and afraid of crying in public (over a sweater!), I left the store without buying. Until my illness, I hadn't realized how stressful it is to drive a car. The responsibility of controlling that large machine, the all-sense alertness, the intensity of concentration left me weak.

Walking was my way back to health. Two house lengths at first, then four, then to the corner, and then—a cause for celebration—all around the block. The daily advice from each member of my family going off to a busy world outside was a loving "take care of yourself." After seven months of this, I decided I needed some purpose in life in addition to self-preservation. Since school is my answer to everything I enrolled in a course, chosen not by subject or even teacher, but by location, time of day and ease of parking. Even with those carefully selected pluses, I stood at the building door that September morning, wondering if I could do it. I forced myself to go up the stairs to class, not knowing what a reward awaited my courage. The class was one in art history, the teacher, so enthused about the subject that she inspired us all. For three years I arranged my schedule around whatever class she taught.

With the advent of art history, my life began to return to normal. I was determined that the heart attack would not "completely change my life," as so many predicted. Of course, there have been some adaptations. I always carry nitro-glycerin pills, because it would be foolish not to. I make sure to walk or swim regularly. I carry heavy packages up one flight of stairs, but never two. Otherwise I have rarely felt restricted or discouraged. Once, traveling in Scotland with my daughter and her roommate, we went to climb the low hills near Aberfeldy. Going up I became very out of breath, and, remembering how far I was from home, decided I had to stop. I went down the hill as the girls continued up, but I turned my head so they wouldn't see my tears of disappointment. On a steep hill, I have felt sudden chest pain and have had to stop. Otherwise the heart attack is behind me.

It is not fully behind my husband. He doesn't try to overprotect me and shows no worry. But two things reflect the strain of those days on the bench outside the cardiac care unit. When we travel, he always packs a blood pressure kit in his suitcase; and if I am late he begins to panic. If I announce, "I'm not well," my instant next sentence always defines the illness: "My head is killing me," or "I think it's the flu." I do this to put his mind at ease.

Some years after the heart attack we were assigned to the U.S. Embassy in Iceland, and the story completes itself with two events from our years there. First, I had my fifty-fourth birthday. While stretching in bed that April birthday morning, a feeling of relief flowed through me. "I'm fifty-four. I made it." Only at that moment did I realize the worry I had carried all the previous year. My mother had died at fifty-three of a stroke.

And later in the year, I was able to put my illness to use. When my Icelandic language became good enough, I worked with several women's groups in the country. As a member of the Icelandic Red Cross, I helped regularly in the city hospital, and one morning found myself there counseling a heart attack patient worried about her future. Part of me stepped outside the scene and watched in astonishment. Here I was, in a language I really knew only partially, giving medical advice—certainly not my field of expertise—to a worried woman. Still, I thought, I was certainly able to say life does go on and can go on very actively. She was at the moment of needing encouragement, and I was in a position to give it. My heart and I had come full circle.

Ambassador?

At our house the summer of 1972 was several months long. We lived in suspension with our lives on hold.

In the spring, my husband had received word that the State Department wanted him to be the United States Ambassador to Iceland. After appropriate meetings of senior officers in the Department, his name had been sent to the White House for consideration. There it was balanced against a political nominee, an insurance company executive to whom President Nixon owed a favor.

A few months earlier, the then U.S. Ambassador in Iceland, himself a political appointee, wrote to President Nixon that the political situation in Iceland had changed and that he could no longer handle it. He said it was important to send an experienced career officer to lead the Embassy. Otherwise, he wrote, he was afraid the strategic anti-submarine base located in Iceland would be closed. As a man of honor, he resigned so that a career officer could replace him.

Despite this advice, the White House staff, including Haldeman and Ehrlichman, urged appointment of the insurance executive. State Department countered by stressing how important it was to send someone with experience. Apparently when Nixon read the resumés of both men, the name "Fred Irving" caught his eye. "Is he the man who was in Educational and Cultural Affairs at State, the one who once sent me a message asking if I thought he had rocks in his head?"

A year earlier Fred had been the Senior Deputy in Educational and Cultural Affairs, a policy making job, often filled by a political appointee. When pressed to name his political affiliation, which no Foreign Service officer is supposed to reveal, Fred had refused to answer. The questioner then modified the request to ask if Fred would state that, if given that job, he would do nothing to embarrass the President or the office of the President. Fred asked that his exact words be sent as his reply. "Please ask the President if he thinks I have rocks in my head." It was that remark that Nixon remembered. "We need a man who will speak his mind. He's the one." Back from the California White House came word that Fred Irving was the President's choice for Iceland.

State Department was about to submit Fred's nomination to the Senate when that body filibustered. The filibuster was on a political matter that had nothing to do with Iceland, but State felt it best to hold all appointments until the filibuster was settled. The speeches went on all summer.

The delay brought many uncertainties. Three older officers who had held a senior FSO rank longer than had Fred felt they should have first consideration for any ambassadorial post. One of these went to a member of the Senate Foreign Relations Committee to further his own chances, but State Department quickly squelched that development. When the other two tried approaching senior members of the Administration outside of State Department, they also were put aside. All Foreign Service Officers (FSOs) were subject to a promotion panel each year. Under this process, they were gradually promoted up through the ranks from FSO-8 to 7, to 6 and finally up to FSO-1. Each year, the night the promotion lists came out, Fred and I had dinner with our closest Foreign Service friends. Our children still remember our exclamations as we read the lists. "How did HE make it?" or "Good, that promotion is well deserved." Most career officers hoped to make ambassador but for a group of about one hundred and fifty FSO-1s, there were only about a half dozen Chiefs of Mission posts available. It was not an automatic next step.

In June another threat came to Fred's nomination. An assistant to columnist Jack Anderson telephoned to say he had it on good authority that Fred, as a member of the Department's Grievance Committee, had taken part in an action Anderson considered inappropriate, and, unless Fred could prove he had not taken part, the matter would be written up in the next day's column. Anderson's daily "gossip" column in the Washington Post was faithfully read by most government employees. It was not a place you wished to see your own name. After the telephoned threat, Fred tried to reconstruct where he had been on the day of the critical meeting. He phoned the newspaper to learn the exact date and time the meeting was held, and then searched his own records hoping he could prove he had not participated. With a tremendous sigh of relief, he found that the date and even the hour matched exactly the time Fred was anesthetized undergoing back surgery at George Washington University Hospital. He gave the investigative reporter the facts and invited him to check with the hospital and the doctor, whose name Fred offered. "You can be sure I will," answered the Anderson flunkey. We assume he did call and found Fred's version true. There was no mention of the case in the column. We hoped no more snags would arise.

Between the aggressive FSOs and the Anderson incident, we began to get a little paranoid. That summer, our older daughter was among the college "carpetbaggers" who had gone to Michigan to help the Democratic Senate nominee in a widely publicized and highly partisan campaign. I had lent her my car to drive out and to use while there. Suddenly Fred and I had the same thought. If something happened to the car and it came out that the vehicle was owned by a Dorothy Irving, whose husband was being considered for a Nixon ambassadorship—what would the press do with this? Much to Sue's amazement, we phoned her that we needed the car back; we would pay for her to rent one. Furthermore, we said, Rick and Barbara would fly out the next day to pick it up. My car reached home safely, with neither accident nor press coverage. We crossed our fingers and succumbed once more to out-waiting the filibuster.

Our impatience was partly because we wanted the nomination confirmed and settled, and also because we knew all the things we would need to do before leaving for post, none of which could be started until our orders came through. I did go to the Foreign Service Institute for some of the courses they offered. "How to talk through an interpreter," *Look at the principal, not the interpreter.* "How to protect yourself against violence," *If you have one chance for a blow, aim toward the center of your attacker.* "How to keep track of finances in a government residence," etc. I also attended their survey courses on American art, music, history. Whatever I knew in such fields would never be enough.

The things we could not do were meet with the Foreign Buildings people who were in charge of all embassy properties and had drawings of the Reykjavík Residence and samples of furniture fabrics used there. Nor could Fred and I yet meet with the Arts in Embassy Office to choose which of the American art works available we would like to have for use in the public rooms of the Residence. I could, on my own, begin to learn Icelandic, but it seemed a little presumptuous to do that. We could read the latest post report from Iceland. These were available from the Family Briefing Office, and contained such useful knowledge as customs, types of dress, items hard to get at post, seasonal changes, recreation.

We could not take steps to rent our home, nor could we apply for our next passport. These next ones would contain Fred's new rank: Frederick Irving, Ambassador of the United States of America, Dorothy Irving, Wife of the U.S. Ambassador. For our children they would read son or daughter of the Ambassador.

At least our only school decision was easy. Our older two children were in college and graduate school. Barbara, who was about to enter her senior year in high school, would either continue at her present school (if we were not confirmed), or transfer to the high school at the Naval Base in our new country. For myself, I declined a position that would open that fall. In March, the Principal of the school where I tutored asked me to take charge of establishing and administering in-school tutoring programs throughout Montgomery County. In April, Fred's official *agrément* was sent to the government of Iceland. In April, I told my principal I could not take the new position.

Finally, the filibuster ended. It had lasted about six weeks, not six months, as we felt. In late August Fred's name was forwarded to the Senate for their advice and consent. His hearing was scheduled before the Senate Foreign Relations Committee. The day before the hearing, as was customary, he met with a member of the State Department's Congressional Relations Office. Here he met his last roadblock.

Apparently another case involving the Grievance Committee was soon going to come before the Senate. It wasn't going to affect the appointment to Iceland, but it made membership on that committee seem controversial. "If a Senator asks if you served as a member of the Grievance Committee, your answer is 'No,'" Fred was advised. "Of course I won't lie to the Senate, and I won't lie under oath." When the Congressional Relations Officer threatened to have the hearing postponed, Fred said if that happened he would report that he had been urged to lie. He came home furious. His hearing was not postponed.

The next day Senator Fulbright praised Fred's record and asked him many questions about how he would conduct the pending base negotiations. He did not mention the Grievance Committee. Fred answered everything truthfully, including, at one point, saying, "Senator, I don't know the answer to that."

Senator Fulbright was so pleased at Fred's testimony, he urged the committee to approve the nomination immediately and unanimously. "Today I think we have a Foreign Service Officer who tells the truth, a man we can trust." He turned to Fred, "Congratulations! I think the Senate will easily confirm your appointment as Ambassador."

Rebecca

(After Fred's nomination was confirmed by the Senate, we bought our official Ambassadorial stationery and proudly sent samples to our families. Later I learned what my mother-in-law, Rebecca, had done with hers.)

It is the symbolism of the calling card in her apron pocket that I shall never forget. Women of her generation wore dress length, over-the-shoulder aprons when they did their housework, aprons with two pockets in front. Now, every day her right front pocket held this special joy: the engraved card that read "Frederick Irving, Ambassador of the United States of America." Fred was her youngest son. Rebecca could not read the black letters, but she could run her fingers over them and she knew what they said. She would show the card proudly to any neighbor who stopped in.

No one had a better right to be proud. I wondered if she remembered the struggle it had been to keep her family together after her husband died of a burst appendix, misdiagnosed in the hospital. She was thirty-two when he died, left with six children from four to twelve years old. Relatives, interfering, but not helpful, told her she could not raise all those children alone. She would have to divide them up.

"You have no money and no job," they reminded her. "It won't be possible to manage."

To satisfy the most pressing of them, she let herself be taken to visit an orphanage. My husband, at four, the youngest, didn't know the purpose of the visit, but he remembers that dark and gloomy room in a large building. After the visit, his mother declared, "I will keep the children together, and I will manage somehow."

And manage, they did; she, by taking in piecework from a Providence jewelry factory. At night, she sewed snaps and hooks onto watchbands. Her five sons and one daughter remember sitting with her around the kitchen table, sorting the pieces she would need.

As soon as they could, the children took jobs: in the grocery store, at the fruit and vegetable stand, delivering newspapers. My husband's first job, at age six, was removing the outer dirty peelings from onions in one hundred-pound sacks. When he fell asleep at work, the storekeeper paid him twenty-five cents for his time and said that, perhaps, the boy should wait until he was a little older to get a job.

The spotty income was not enough to keep the family from going on welfare.

"We're doing this now," their mother said, "because we must, but when you grow up, you must pay back this country by being good citizens and giving what you can."

Despite the assurance that this was a temporary need, being on welfare was a degrading experience. Every week, the "Welfare Lady" came to the house. My husband remembers her long black dress, long black coat, and a black hat that hid part of her face. She checked on how the week's money had been spent. Rebecca would never lie. One hot summer day she had bought each child an ice cream cone from the truck that drove down the street. Thirty cents for six cones; thirty cents was deducted from the next week's allowance. Another time, to help the boys with their delivery of the heavy Sunday newspapers, their mother bought them a wagon.

"A wagon is a toy," she was told. The cost of the wagon was spread over the next few weeks.

Somehow, Rebecca kept her brood cheerful, unresentful, and raised them all to be honorable people. I cannot conceive of any one of them telling a lie, cheating, or being unkind. This is probably one of the few families I know that doesn't resent paying taxes. It is a feeling that the government is there to help those who need, and we can now do our part, too. The now grown children remember—not happily—that all their clothes were bought too big with the hope that they might last two or more years. They comment on the present pleasure of having something that fits while it is new.

In the early 1940s, the five boys went to war, in the last war that America backed wholeheartedly. The country saw the threat and the evil of Hitler's Nazism, and was united in subduing it. Families who had men—less often women—in the armed services proudly hung a small flag in a front window. On a white background outlined in red, each flag held a blue star for any family member in uniform, a gold star if someone in the family had died in the war. My mother-in-law's flag carried five blue stars. Again those bustling relatives criticized.

"You should never have let them all go. As a widow, you could have kept one home to help you." they scolded.

"And which one would I have kept?" she answered. "They all wanted to serve their country, and I am proud of them." They all went and they all came home.

The country they served was one Rebecca had come to as a child of nine. She, her parents, and eight brothers and sisters had traveled from Eastern Europe to Ellis Island, to Providence, Rhode Island. There, the father found work at Korb's bakery. He was a good worker, and Korb's kept him on, even after he was jailed a day for trying to start a union among the bakers in the shop. I do not know what use he made of his ability to speak four languages. He and his wife, now expecting, decided that in such a large family, one of the children would have to be kept home to help. Rebecca, the most home loving, was chosen; the others went to school. Thus, this giving child never learned to read and write, but she knew what she missed. Her respect for her sisters' education made her too easily swayed by them, and over and over she told her children that they must get as much education as they could. They must study hard and try to go to college.

Like the others, my husband had a full time job from early high school on. Perhaps the fact that he never had time to do all his homework contributed to our friendship, for I often helped him with his Latin and German translations. He thanked me by extra large cones of ice cream at the soda fountain where he worked—until a loud voice from the back room would shout, "Put back the lid. You're giving that customer too much!" During college he continued working forty hours a week and lived at home. By graduate school, he could attend on the G.I. Bill, passed after World War II.

And now, this youngest son had a calling card that read, "Ambassador." Nowhere would it be more important or more valued than it was here in Rebecca's apron pocket.

ICELAND 1972-76

Our First Ambassadorial Post

The Challenge

In the 1970s the United States was still in a period of Cold War with the Soviet Union. Despite efforts to encourage détente, there had been little progress. Iceland became one of the playing fields where this contest was carried on.

Iceland's geographic location made it the ideal place to monitor Soviet nuclear submarines moving into the Atlantic Ocean from the Kola Peninsula in the North. Once in the Atlantic, such subs could release missiles that could reach North and South America and much of The Middle East and Africa. Monitoring of this traffic was the principal task of the U.S Naval Station at Keflavik, which, on arrival, Fred renamed the "NATO Base."

In 1972, Icelandic elections had resulted in formation of a three party coalition government, one of them communist oriented. The coalition's platform included shutting down the Base. Because of that election, the then U.S. Ambassador to Iceland (a political appointee) had resigned, urging that an experienced Foreign Service Officer was needed to resist those in the newly elected Icelandic government who were working to get the Base removed.

Iceland's objection to the Base was not against the Americans, but against having any military stationed on their soil. "If it's going to be anyone, we want the Americans," they said. Iceland, itself, has no military. The country was proud to belong to NATO, and viewed housing the Base as their contribution to that organization. They refused to accept money for the use of their land. "If it is the right thing to do we shall do it. If it is not right, all the money in Fort Knox would not persuade us to continue." Of all the countries where the United States has had bases, Iceland stands alone as the country that would accept no rent for use of their land.

The Icelanders who wanted the Base closed were chiefly concerned about the threat to their country's culture. Iceland is properly proud and protective of its history, its literature and its language. Individual Icelanders put great value on all of these factors; they do not want to be "taken over" by another country's culture. In a land of two hundred and sixty thousand people, the three thousand servicemen and their families at the Base could be seen as such a threat.

The western nations hoped that the Base would stay; the Soviets hoped to see it thrown out. In an effort to influence Iceland, the USSR had enlarged its Embassy staff to seventy-seven members, all Soviet citizens. They said it was because they had so much trade with Iceland. The U.S. Embassy had eleven Americans and thirteen Icelanders. During our four years in Reykjavík, Moscow sent three different ambassadors. One ambassador's wife told me that if her husband got the Base to close he would be rewarded with Paris for his next assignment. She was looking forward to it. They did not go to Paris.

Arrival in Iceland

I loved Iceland from the moment our plane touched down at Keflavik airport. Although, certainly on that first day, I had no idea how much more I would come to love the country during our four years there. American friends who had visited Iceland alerted us that the road from the airport to the capital city of Reykjavík was rather bleak. "Remember, Iceland is where the astronauts trained to walk on the moon," warned one. Another advised, "When you leave the airport, just close your eyes until you reach the city." I was much too curious about my new home to close my eyes, and soon much too fascinated by the new scenery to want to blink and miss any of it. As a woman who had loved trees all of her life and who had spent many happy summers in the forests of Maine, I found this treeless landscape was surprisingly appealing. The road to the capital was two lanes wide; to either side stretched fields of lava. It lay in mounds, in crevices, in gullies, on low hills. Mosses of many colors and small shrubs grew on it. On our right, the low landscape stretched to the horizon; to our left a shorter expanse reached to the sea. On the seaward side a few small shelters nestled in the lava rocks. "Summer houses," answered our driver, "holiday houses for people who live in the city." The cloudless morning sky was endless. In preparation for our trip I had read much about Iceland and knew of the belief many there held in the presence of "Little People." Seeing this lava filled landscape made me feel how easily such a belief could develop.

In addition to being enchanted by the countryside, I was intrigued by the language of this land. In the lounge of Kennedy Airport as we awaited the delayed departure of our overnight plane, I had heard two young Icelandic women talking with each other. I liked the rhythm and intonation of their speech. On this first trip into the city, I asked our driver for the Icelandic names of things we passed, and again liked the Icelandic sound of his answers. I noted, too, a lift in his shoulders at my expressed interest in learning the language soon. Before we reached the capital, I mastered "*Gerid svo vel*," and "*Takka ydur fyrir*" (Please and Thank you.)

We rode past the fishing village of Kopavogur and soon approached the capital. Off to the right we saw a larger than life statue of a woman bending to lift two pails of water. *The Water Carrier* was sculpted by an Icelandic artist we would soon know. It had been placed in the area where women had once drawn and carried water for the citizens of the city. When pipes were to be installed, the water carriers went on a futile strike; their usefulness was at an end. They were memorialized here.

After about forty-five minutes we came into Reykjavík. On the incline to our left stretched the old city cemetery where, I was told, at Christmastime graves were decorated with lights, as was the rest of the city. "Shouldn't the dead enjoy Christmas, too?" Icelanders would say. Within the city, narrow streets were lined with white cement houses two to three stories high. With their corrugated tin roofs, painted red, green, brilliant blue, they gave a postcard look to the city. A few old houses had walls of the corrugated tin, and a few were sheathed with wood boards, here placed vertically, not horizontally as in New England. In many front windows I saw plants set on wide sills between window and sheer curtain. Later I would hear neighbors commenting to each other about, "How well your geranium is doing this summer." When we turned onto Laufasvegur, the street which would become our new address, we could see, halfway down the block, the American flag flying over the door of number twenty-three.

The Ambassador's Residence and the Embassy office were in two connected buildings. Like most of the houses they opened directly onto the sidewalk. A large double door led to the office part, or chancery; a smaller wooden door opened into the front hall of the Residence. On that first entering floor was a coatroom, a guest bath, and, through another door, a large kitchen plus a bedroom and sitting room for household help if one had any. I walked up the stairs to the main floor to be greeted with sunshine. All the rooms had large windows, and I immediately liked the brightness, the light of the house. On the top floor were four bedrooms, three baths and the study my husband and I would use. Here, too, there was a feeling of light and cheerfulness.

Our plane had arrived in Iceland at seven in the morning. As is customary for the arrival of a new Ambassador, most of the senior American staff had come to the airport to welcome us. I sympathized with a couple who had brought along two very young children, for I realized that in order to meet the plane, they had left Reykjavík before six. We ourselves had been up all night. After an overnight flight, we never knew whether to go to bed immediately on arrival or to stay up for the whole day and hope to be soon adjusted to the new time schedule. One Christmas our college son just stayed on U.S. time during his week's vacation. He had term papers to write and wrote them at Icelandic night, U.S. day; he never had to readjust when he returned to the States in January. For us, that first day, we had asked to have a morning coffee arranged at the Residence so that we would have a chance to meet the staff and their families right away. Later in the day we were driven around our new city, and then by nightfall, even with the excitement of arrival, our energy ran out and we fell asleep.

There was much to do that first week. Our younger daughter was to start her senior high school year at the NATO Base School at Keflavik. Department of Defense schools overseas range from excellent to far less than excellent; this one fell in the "far less than excellent" category. At the end of her senior year, our Merit Scholar was to say that her most interesting subject at the Base school had been typing. My husband had to get settled in his job and make his government calls, and I had to learn where things were, how to manage the household, and make my calls. Usually an Embassy residence comes with a staff of one or many, depending on its size. The Reykjavík residence is one of the smallest in the Foreign Service, but it was unusual to have no one there to help us. This would not have been a problem, except that certain activities were expected of me right away. After I called on wives of other ambassadors and of Icelandic officials, they returned the courtesy by calling on me. Every morning after clearing up from breakfast, I arranged the Residence tea tray with its Embassy china and silver, and placed it on a shelf in the pantry, ready, should anyone stop in.

I was also busy that first week learning the location of shops for bread, milk, and groceries. A dairy and small grocery were the closest shops, and until I explored further, we had a rather limited diet. We laughed when our college junior sent us his weekly menu. This was his first year living outside of a dormitory, and we had been concerned that he be sure to eat well. When his list of meals arrived we wrote back that he was doing much better than we were!

He was so concerned he said he considered bringing out a suitcase of food on his Thanksgiving visit. But by then we had been in Iceland eight weeks; we were well settled and could offer him nourishment and city tours with equal assurance.

Home(s)

"Remember, this is your home." I smile at our children as we move in. Our children lift their eyebrows and smile at each other. I hear the whisper, "Except, of course, for the holy government rug."

This will be the third time our children have lived in housing owned and furnished by the U.S. Government, housing that goes with their father's job. They know what it means. They know the dining room is their dining room unless we're having a dinner party. The living room is theirs unless their father or I have guests there. On the Fourth of July the house will entertain scores of countrymen they have never met before. The children know, also, that their bedrooms are theirs only until a bed is needed for a visiting Washington VIP. Still, I am correct. It's the only home we have just now, so it is indeed their home.

The beautiful furniture in the house is ours to live with and care for during our stay and to return in the same condition as we found it. Recognizing the need for this care, our children, three moves ago, coined the phrase, "the holy government rug."

They should have appreciated the rug. It was one of the few things they didn't have to help me count. Within a week of arrival, I was required to identify and sign for every item in the house on a multi-page inventory. Here in Iceland, the children could help me.

"Mom, it says sixty soup spoons. There are only fifty-four." The spoons are lined up on the dining room table.

"Put down fifty-four. Washington wants to know what is missing." Each Embassy Residence has silver, china, crystal for six more people than would fit at a sit-down dinner.

"Mom, tell me again which are the glasses for red wine and which for white?" This from the daughter lifting down the lovely crystal crested with the seal of the United States.

"How about this tablecloth? It measures one hundred and six inches. Should I check off the one hundred inch one or the one hundred and fourteen inch?"

There were tablecloths for varying lengths of the dining room table using one, two, three, or four leaves. Several months later, tired of unrolling each cloth to find which would fit the extension for the evening, I embroidered two, three or four small circles in the corner of each—designating how many leaves it would cover. Measuring and labeling seemed a nuisance until I talked with the Mexican Ambassador's wife who told me they had to provide their own table linens at every post. "For all those differing tables!" I thought.

After the dining room, the rest of the inventory seemed simple. Pillowcases and blankets, sheets and towels were quickly counted. In the large kitchen we whipped through saucepans, potato mashers, kettles, and trays. Big pieces of furniture were the easiest. We had only to locate the E39584 or E27361 stenciled on the bottom or back of each couch, lamp, chair, or bed.

When our own furniture arrived a few weeks later, it too had numbers—red labels placed by Paxton Movers in Washington: P234, P110. With Paxton, a red label identified something going overseas; blue marked pieces going into storage during our absence.

With the arrival of our own things, the lovely hotel atmosphere became more homelike. The Van Gogh print that always hangs over our fireplace found a wall near the fireplace here. The four paintings my husband had made us one Christmas hung across from it. The Constitution, which always greets people in our front hall, was put in this latest hall. Near it went Susan's sampler. Her Little Women dolls were placed on the wide windowsill along the curved staircase. My own small desk fit nicely between the two front living room windows. Special books found homes in the bookcase or on a coffee table. Rick's framed photos, Barbara's candlesticks went in the dining room. A favorite vase from my parent's home represented my childhood. The cranberry scoop magazine rack suggested New Englanders now lived here. It began to feel like home.

So much like home that when, after four years of building memories there, it was time to return to Washington, it was like leaving home to go home.

Iceland 1972-76

During those four years our youngest had followed the others back to college, and the departure inventory had to be made by me and the Administrative Officer of the Embassy. I missed the children. But I reported to them that everything was intact, and I was happy to state that the holy government rug still looked great.

Now that we are home to stay, a few red Paxton labels remain. You won't see them if you visit me—they are underneath. I have left them on purpose. They tell me this piece of furniture was part of our lives in many places. It is as if the small desk is saying, "I, too, served abroad. I once sat in a living room in Iceland and a study in Jamaica." The Pennsylvania Dutch rocker looks as good in Belmont as it did in Vienna. Seeing those pieces reminds me of the places they've been, of the people who have passed them or admired them. Their traveled presence gives deeper meaning to my words, "This is your home."

Do you speak ...?

Icelandic? Yes, I do. And it wasn't easy. As part of a Foreign Service family, I always tried to learn something of the language of each new temporary home abroad. In our other assignments, this wasn't so hard. When living in Vienna, I found my high school and college German gave me a good start on the Austrian version of that language. My American English was related to the English of New Zealand, although I did keep meeting surprises there: "homely" meant homelike, not unattractive; "bloody" was never used, even if you were trying to describe to the doctor the appearance of your four-year-old's ear the day after her tonsillectomy. But, basically the languages were the same. When we were going to Jamaica, a Jamaican friend told me, "Just remember, Dorothy, the ac*cen*t will be on a dif*fer*ent syl*lab*le." How often in Kingston I thought of her advice. Until my first hearing of a multi-syllabic word, I had no idea how it would come out.

But Icelandic was new to me. Full of optimism, I purchased a copy of *Teach Yourself Icelandic* and was happily to chapter two when I met the convenient tourist phrase, "Where is the railroad station, please?" Iceland prides itself on having moved directly from the horse to the airplane. There have never been any railroads or any stations. I decided *Teach Yourself Icelandic* could stay behind in America. Surely, once in Iceland, I could find a teacher, and I could do what immigrants to America had long done—learn from the newspaper.

The paper was not helpful. In Icelandic, everything is declined, even personal names. Four endings singular, and four plural. I picked out the name of the Foreign Minister in one article, but never saw it again, not realizing I was, indeed, seeing it but not recognizing in its second form, not yet knowing that Águstson and Áugustsonar were the same man. Clearly, a teacher was necessary. The course at the university was out because my time was unpredictable, but the college suggested a language teacher who would come to our home. A very learned linguistic professor arrived; he spent the first hour emphasizing how important it was to understand fricatives. After three weeks of fricatives (I still do not know what they are), and no new words, the professor and I parted company.

I made a few more attempts at finding a teacher, and soon came to the three approaches, which would serve me so well. First, a recent university graduate, an English major, came to help me twice a week. I learned much about both Iceland and its language from her. We still correspond in a dual language. Secondly, I was told of a woman who might help me read the old sagas, something I was eager to do. Each Monday afternoon I spent two hours with Frú Gerda, while we read the old literature. Because Icelanders have kept their language so pure, even a beginner could, with help, read the early writings. The difference between old and new Icelandic is not as great as the difference that exists between modern English and the language of Beowulf.

And, thirdly, I learned from the children on our street. The Embassy in Reykjavík is on a narrow city street with homes, shops, and apartments along it. One day while listening to language tapes on the terrace, I noticed two Icelandic children looking over the wall at me. I invited them in and they became the core of seven children who used to come by, listen to me read children's stories and unhesitatingly correct my accent. I can still hear the small boy who lived across the street saying urgently, "Nei, Frú Irving, not 'r', 'e-r-r.'" This same small boy and I had a discussion one day about the two feather pens on my desk. I told him they were copies of ones used by Thomas Jefferson, "a very famous American in the old days." "Nei, Frú Irving," the boy replied, "not Thomas Jefferson, Snorri Sturluson" (an author of early Icelandic writings). The pens became and have remained, one from Thomas Jefferson and one from Snorri Sturluson.

Three of the children who came lived in an apartment where their parents ran a furrier repair shop; one lived with her family over their hardware store on the other side of the street. It was she, who, when I went to invite the mothers to coffee, called upstairs, "Momma, the good lady is here." The two boys who had been leaning over the terrace wall lived across from us on the top floor of a multi-family dwelling.

At the time of President Nixon's visit, they were playing at their fourth floor window. Their toy gun caught the eye of the Secret Service agent standing with my husband and me at our front door awaiting the President's arrival. Almost before I realized the agent had left my side on the street, his face appeared in that top window between the two boys.

Encouraged by brownies and cookies, the children came regularly, sometimes when it wasn't a language class, and always if I'd been away. We knew it was the children if the front doorbell rang and there was no face tall enough to show through the door's high windows. Once, tired from the overnight flight back from the United States, I asked my husband to go to the door and tell the children I would see them tomorrow. "I think you'd better come," he said. There they stood with a bouquet of flowers, proudly explaining that each of them had given money to pay for it. My husband was always amused when the group came to the door and asked if "Mrs. Irving can come out." "…to play," he added.

And so I came to know Icelandic. I learned it because I wanted to, because I liked the sound of it, and because I was interested in the language of this land that so treasured the written word; this land with the highest literacy rate in the world, where the best Christmas present is a book, one of the many new ones published each year, or a new edition of one of the old sagas.

The sagas are such a part of daily life, that even at official dinners, people will argue over whether a hero should have acted as he did; so much a part of daily life that they are used as a barometer of busyness. The young university graduate who helped me, wrote me after her second child was born, "I've been so busy with the babies, I haven't even had time to read *Njala* (the most famous saga) this year." How many of us say casually in a letter, "I haven't even had time to read Whitman or Twain this year?" Iceland so valued language that when the country adopted TV, the opening program was not an extravaganza, a musical group or a nature film. It presented their Nobel Prize winning author, Haldor Laxness, seated in a chair reading from a book open on his lap. Icelanders so protected their language that instead of adopting the international "TV," they called the device, *sjónvarp*, Icelandic for "throw forth a picture."

Iceland 1972-76

And so I learned Icelandic. Because the language is spoken by only the two hundred and sixty thousand inhabitants of that proud country and by their descendants overseas it is not often learned by a foreigner, and certainly not necessary. Most Icelanders speak at least two other languages. But learning it opened many doors, not only for my own deep pleasure, but also in the hearts of Icelanders. After a concert my second year there, I told one of the performers that the music had been beautiful. My simple declarative statement brought the warm response, "You know our language so well." With a reception like that, how could I not keep on?

Soon most of Iceland knew I spoke their language. On a camping trip with our children, I stopped at a small restaurant in eastern Iceland. The waitress greeted us warmly, "You're the American who speaks Icelandic," she smiled. My respect for their language and customs helped many Icelanders feel more comfortable about the United States, and thus about the presence of the NATO Base.

At our farewell dinner, the Foreign Minister complimented my husband for always being honest and a man of integrity in all their dealings and for treating Iceland as an equal nation. Then he turned to me. "And Dorothy," he said, "furthered good relations between our two countries at a time of stress, and she loved us enough to learn our difficult language." It was a moving goodbye.

When I returned to Boston and went job hunting, the bottom line of my resumé read: "Language: Icelandic"

It did not open many doors, but I would not remove it.

Learning from the Top-Names in Iceland

(Only the names of Kristrún and her family are actual)

"I think you know my mother," the young woman said as she introduced herself to me at the Reykjavík teachers' conference. She was attending as a teacher from an Icelandic school; I, as an American teacher, now living in Iceland. The conference, sponsored by the U.S. Information Service, was held at their library in Reykjavík.

The young woman gave her name: Kristrún Ólafsdóttir, and I searched my mind for any motherly person I had met with the last name, Ólafsdóttir. My husband and I had then been in Iceland only a few weeks, but had met many people in that short time.

Kristrún and I walked down the stairs to the room where the opening session would be held. I felt she was smiling inside at my obvious searching for her mother's name. I was not smiling on the inside, but I tried to appear relaxed on the outside.

Just before we entered the lecture room, Kristrún spoke. With twinkling eyes, she said softly, "My father is the Prime Minister." Oops! My husband was the newly arrived American Ambassador to Iceland. We had indeed met the Prime Minister and his wife. It was hardly the best diplomatic introduction to a country that I did not connect the names, that I did not know that in Iceland the last names of parents and children do not match.

I had not been prepared for the system of Icelandic names. Everyone is the son or daughter of the father in the family. Kristrún Ólafsdóttir was the daughter of Ólafur Jóhannesen, then the Prime Minister. Kristrún's mother was Dóra Gudbjartsdóttir, Dóra, daughter of Gudbjartur. A woman keeps her birth name all her life. Family names as we know them in the United States do not exist in Iceland.

Iceland's use of names was a constant challenge for my American mind. When I met a woman at coffee, say a Sigrún Pétursdóttir, I had no way of finding her in the phone book, should I wish to follow up the contact. My great support in this effort was an Icelandic woman employed at the Embassy. The morning after meeting someone, I would telephone Thórunn, describe where and when I had met my new acquaintance, mention anything particular we had talked about. In a few minutes Thórunn would tell me, "Oh, Mrs. Irving, she is the wife of Birgir Gústafsson, who is…" and she would name his profession "Just a minute and I'll give you her address." Thórunn was always correct.

It was not only with the Prime Minister's daughter that I had shown my ignorance of Icelandic custom. I had invited to the teachers' conference an Icelandic teacher, a woman I had met in those first weeks. While filling out my own name card, I printed one for her: "Mrs. Jón Gudmundsson." I was careful to put the correct accent over the "o" in Jón, but Mrs. Gudmundsson did not wear her card. I realized why when I saw the return address on a thank you note she sent me, "Vigdis Pétursdóttir, wife of Jón." She clearly was not Mrs. Jón Gudmundsson. I never called her that again.

I might have been warned by my experience at the Reykjavík library. Our first week in Iceland I had walked around the block to the city library to apply for a card. When I handed my form to the receptionist: "Name: Mrs. Frederick Irving. Address: 23 Laufasvegur," she looked up with interest. "Is Frederick a woman's name in America? Here we use it only for men." Since that day I have been Dorothy Irving.

The double names were a further challenge when putting place cards around for a dinner party. In diplomatic life, seating is done by rank, which husband and wife share. The first ranking male guest sits at the right of the hostess; his spouse sits at the right of the host. The second guest and spouse sit at the left, and so it goes down the table. I either knew in advance or learned from the Embassy the comparative ranks of our guests, so the order of seating them was neither a problem nor a choice. The challenge was those non-matching names. Until I knew more people well, I did not automatically know that a Kristín Helgadóttir and a Björn Sigurdursson were husband and wife and must be seated in corresponding positions. To help me arrange the table, I would write two long lists on a yellow pad: twelve husbands' names in one column, twelve wives listed across from them, the -sons on one side, the -dóttirs on the other. I carried the pad and the place cards into the dining room, and moved from side to side around the table, placing one pair of cards at a time. Finally, to be sure everyone matched and each couple had corresponding seats, I circled the table twice, pad in hand. It is true most people might not mind, but one never knew who would take offense at being seated higher or lower than his spouse. Also, I felt at the home of the American Ambassador, things should be done correctly. I was later told that Icelandic women did not expect to have their proper Icelandic names used at foreign embassies, but I was also told how very much they appreciated the fact that at the American Embassy it was done. They said we were the only embassy that did.

At one of the last dinners we went to at Government House before leaving Iceland, I felt I had finally mastered the names. After the meal, a group of Icelanders was sitting informally in an upstairs living room discussing relatives and family. Icelanders know these things and take them very seriously. To my surprise, I found I could enter the conversation. I knew whose cousin was whose, and at what farm in Iceland their ancestors had settled. Suddenly it all fell into place. Both I and the Icelanders present were delighted at my participation. One said, "Dorothy really knows us and understands us, you know."

The Prime Minister's wife entered the room in time to hear the remark. She and I smiled at each other in silent understanding. She had never been angry at my early gaffe with her name, and whenever she expressed her pleasure at my adjustment to Icelandic customs, I would smile and answer, "As for names, I always remember that I learned it at the top." It was a thought we shared at that moment in Government House.

Cold War Incident

During the Cold War period when we in the United States considered our balance of power with the Soviet Union, there was one weapon we frequently overlooked, namely a particular Soviet government aptitude for doing the wrong thing at the wrong time—and doing it loudly! True, we do not entirely lack this ability in our own country, but there were indications that the Soviets seemed to have a special knack for it.

In the early 1970s in Iceland, the government, then 20 percent Communist-leaning, was making moves to eject the important NATO Base from their country. In an effort to change Icelandic attitudes and thus keep the Base, the United States sent out a career diplomat (my husband) whose one instruction was, "Save the Base." One can only guess at the instructions Moscow gave its Ambassador to Reykjavík that same year.

Dealing with the Soviets in Reykjavík was always interesting, sometimes amusing; sometimes they helped our side. The amusing times came in the exchange of calls all embassies make with each other. We never discussed politics at such visits, but rather holiday customs, foods, etc. When I described American Thanksgiving to the wife of a new Soviet ambassador, she told me that Thanksgiving originated in Russia, as did apple pie, and pumpkin pie. A few weeks after her call on me, I met the same wife at a dinner given by the President of Iceland. There, I heard her tell the President that the Icelandic horse, of which the citizens are extremely proud, the horse that saw them through the pre-motorized era, is really from Russia. Iceland's President took the news as graciously as I had accepted the origin of Thanksgiving.

Because of their reputation for spying and because of the known presence of KGB officers in their Residence, I always emptied my coat pockets before attending any function at the Soviet Embassy.

Guests entered on the ground floor, left their coats in a dark coatroom supervised by three heavy, non-communicative men, and then went upstairs to the event. At our first dinner there, my husband, pursuing the non controversial subject of food, asked the Ambassador's wife from which part of Russia various of the foods had come. "I really have no idea," she said. "I didn't plan the menu. This is what Moscow told us to serve when the American Ambassador and his wife come to dinner."

We were often made aware how little choice or freedom the Russian representatives had.

A group of Communist-oriented students at the University of Iceland asked the U.S. and the USSR embassies to send speakers to a discussion group they were hosting. My husband designated our two junior officers. When they went to him for advice, he told them to tell the truth. "You know America. Answer their questions as well as you can." The Soviets sent two senior officers. After the event our officers returned to say the two Russians who took part had refused to answer several questions; they said they had not been briefed by their Ambassador on those matters. The Icelandic student hosts saw quite a contrast to our open and freewheeling officers.

On a sadder note, there was in Reykjavík a small American school for our youngest Embassy children, open to anyone else who wished to come. A kindergartner from the Russian Embassy was sent to start to learn American English. She enjoyed the school, and they enjoyed her. I saw her in several plays there. The following year, although her parents were still in Reykjavík, the child did not return. "She is at home with her grandmother," explained her mother without a smile. The child had been too happy in the school, and the Soviet government had kept her in Moscow as insurance that her parents would return home.

In time, it was our turn to host the current Soviet couple at our home for dinner (we had a series of three such couples during our tour). Our dinner soon became gossip all over Reykjavík. The Icelanders on our guest list were all staunchly pro-American and pro-Base. The evening moved along pleasantly and was not remarkable until we moved into the living room for after dinner coffee. As we sipped our coffee, the Soviet Ambassador's wife complained loudly to the American Ambassador that she could no longer get her favorite American programs from the Base television. In this "lonely city, this isolated country" she needed these programs. "I used to be able to see them. What has happened?" she demanded of Fred.

"We have shielded the signal," Fred replied, "Iceland asked us to do this so that American television would not be broadcast nightly into Icelandic homes."

"And you did what they asked?" questioned Mrs. USSR.

"Iceland is an independent country, and we are their guests," Fred answered. "If the Icelandic government asks me to turn down the Base TV signal, I must try to do it."

"You are the American Ambassador," she declared. "You don't have to do what Iceland says." At that point her husband interrupted her. There was a rapid Russian exchange between Mr. and Mrs. Soviet Ambassador and a sudden silence and alert listening from the Icelanders present.

"Iceland," she persisted "is just a little country. The United States is a big country. You don't have to do what they want." She stood up. "If *we* were in charge here, we wouldn't listen to them. We would grind them under our feet like this." She demonstrated a grinding heel on our living room carpet, and then sat down.

A vibrant silence followed. Fred and I let it hang in the air until general conversation resumed and the evening ended.

By the next afternoon much of Iceland knew about the grinding heel. We ourselves never repeated the story. But we heard it often from the Icelanders who had been present, and even more often from many who had not been there.

Saving the Base was a long and unsure effort. We likened it to putting a finger in the dike. As each new threat arose sometimes it was my husband's finger or that of another officer. Sometimes I was the one who could stop the danger. On this night at our house it seemed as if the Soviet Ambassador's wife had inserted her finger to strengthen our dike.

Northern Winter

It was ten thirty on an August night in Reykjavík, when I knew winter was coming. The day had been mild—even now, in the evening, a thin sweater was warm enough—but when I went to bed I had to turn on the lights. This encroaching darkness signaled winter.

This was my second year in Iceland, and I had been through a complete cycle of seasons. I had seen the hours of sunlight grow and decrease by minutes each day, by over half an hour each week, by remarkable changes at the end of each month. I knew what this ten thirty darkness meant.

In June there had been light around the clock. Not the brilliant sunshine of noon, but enough light to hold the annual midnight golf tournament at a course outside of Reykjavík. In June we were never tired, and no darkening sky alerted my American brain that it was time to go to bed. When President Nixon and President Pompidou of France met in Iceland that month, onlookers lined the night streets at eleven to watch the two leaders return from their dinner meeting, the motorcades clearly visible to the waving crowd. One Sunday in June our high school daughter asked when she should be home from an all day picnic. "Before dark," I answered, and we both laughed at the number of days that would pass before we saw darkness. In June, one night, we watched the sunset out of our west-facing windows, lingering to see its last colors in the sky. We turned to the eastern windows where dawn's first light was brightening the horizon. From west to east I felt safe in the engulfing hand of sunshine.

But now, in August, darkness at ten thirty meant days were beginning to shorten. By December, there would be only a few hours of soft light between noon and three. The winter sun is so low on the horizon it illuminates objects from the side. Familiar buildings and their shadows become new to the eye. In the heated corner of the city lake, where ducks swim and are fed all year round, the sun's lateral rays reach under the layers of feathers, showing more depth than revealed by summer's overhead light. On New Year's Day, as we walk into the government's midday reception for the diplomatic corps, our shadows stretch long across the snow, and the snow itself reflects new colors from the underlighting. Reykjavík's smokeless sky does nothing to haze light and colors. The northern light painters seek in studios, the changing angle of light, the smog-free sky, was this why Iceland was a land of painters, always trying to capture the special beauty of their country?

Throughout the country, Icelanders affectionately called the days of December and January the "short days." It became a period I looked forward to each year. Homes in Iceland are warmly furnished, with shelves of books, one or more paintings of the beloved lava countryside. In the "short days" the feeling of warmth was enhanced by the use of candles on tables, buffets, wall brackets, pianos. Artists made candleholders of shaped iron, ceramic with lava decorations, ceramic in strong blues, greens, or shades of red, often with candles to match.

When the wall sconces and the table candles were glowing, I felt an increased warmth in the home and an increased closeness to the friends I was visiting. Over a cup of candle-lit coffee one afternoon my hostess first told me the story of her daughter who had died too young. I had seen a photograph on earlier, brighter visits, but the story came out now. On a morning candle-lit visit, a friend described her father's increasing forgetfulness and her deep worry about it. Over candles I learned of an expected baby and of the joys of a child's sudden success. The closeness of these occasions made me wonder if it is impossible to be fake or false when conversing by daytime candlelight. Fakery and falseness are not part of the Icelandic character. Is there a link to the short days?

In one northern town, valleyed between two mountains, the short days mean days of darkness. The low winter sun illuminates the sky briefly, but it can not reach homes in the valley below. When the rays of dawn first shine clearly on the tips of the western mountain, it is a day of rejoicing and celebration. The moving rays will creep downward into summer with each new day.

In Reykjavík, too, after the turn of the year, days begin to lengthen, until suddenly there comes an evening when we leave home for a dinner and it is still daylight. We exclaim about it. Bundled in coats, scarves and gloves, we know this progressing light moving into our day points to summer. It is the sister of my August evening.

In the States, we measure winter by many standards. Television's weather forecasters would inundate us with ever more details and symbols. In Iceland we knew that winter came when the sun shortened its daily visit and left when the hours of daylight again lengthened. In Iceland we forecast by the hours of the sun.

In a book of Icelandic folk songs on my piano over half the titles include the words for spring, summer, sun—often, blessed sun or welcome sun. By its side, my Jamaican songbook sings of blessed shade and the cool of the morning.

Winter Sports

My first winter in Iceland I didn't swim out of doors. When I drove by Reykjavík's pools, I could see that many people were swimming. I knew the pools were warmed by underground springs (the same hot spring water that, piped into our home, heated the house). But, I thought, maybe one had to be born to this.

The second year, I decided to try it. To mix my water metaphors, I took the plunge and I was hooked. Icelandic friends guided me through my first visit: the dressing rooms for undressing, the required pre-pool shower—*au naturel*—the pulling on of bathing suit over wet body, and then the sixty-foot outdoor walk that stretched from warm shower room to warm pool. On a January day, particularly a windy January day, it was a long sixty feet. But, just as I forgot Iceland's rain when the sun came out, I forgot that cold walk as soon as I reached the pool. The water felt wonderful—relaxing and stimulating—and winter muscles were glad to be stretched. Everything below the water was warm: above the water my required bathing hat kept my head warm—an advantage over men whose uncovered hair sometimes showed icicles. After swimming, I felt warm for the day, often leaving my coat on the seat next to me in the car as I drove home.

In time I even used the pools' outdoor dressing rooms. These areas, protected by four walls, were open to the sky above. It was invigorating to rub dry and dress there—invigorating to body and to spirit. If I can swim and dress outside in January, what can I not do? Over the years of their history, Iceland's people met volcanoes, lava flows, long dark winters, and they swam outside year round. No wonder Haldor Laxness had called them, "Independent People."

Once I had started, I swam regularly, usually at nine in the morning with a group of Icelandic friends. We went either to the Olympic sized pool on the east side of town or the smaller, older one on the west side near the ocean. Because Icelanders had strong loyalty to one or the other of the pools, I let my friends choose our destination. I was often asked my own choice, but to this day that preference is something known only to me. I did find it interesting that most of the women I swam with at one pool were members of one major political party (one knew these things in Iceland); at the second pool, my companions were from the major opposition party.

The day I was startled by the radio announcement no friends were with me. Unable to join the group in the morning, I had gone alone at noontime. On my third lap I heard a voice speaking over the pool's public address system, something I had never heard before. I speak some Icelandic, but the rapidity of the words, the echo of the PA system, and my tight bathing cap made it difficult for me to understand what was being said. I lifted the cap off one ear to listen. Was it an alarm? Were we being asked to vacate the pool? A quick glance showed the other swimmers continuing calmly. An immediate re-take glance confirmed that the other swimmers were all male. Mine was the only bathing hat in sight. Perhaps the announcement was saying this hour is reserved for men and that any woman should leave. Was my noontime presence offending Iceland, its national culture? Would people know I was an American? Was I embarrassing the Embassy? A third, very furtive, glance showed no one pointing or even looking my way. No longer relaxed, I finished my swim and left. I later learned that what I had heard had been the noontime news broadcast daily all over the country, including at the swimming pools.

A few days later I easily understood the language I heard spoken at the pool's edge: American English. A city tour bus had brought its passengers to see this winter custom of Iceland. The guide was explaining to her warmly dressed American guests the strange habits of these Icelanders.

"I could never do that," shivered a Texan voice.

"It looks colder than Lake Erie," answered western New York State.

"Dorothy, tell them who you are," whispered one of my companions in Icelandic.

"No, let's not," I whispered back and we continued swimming.

Before the tour group left I heard a few cameras click. Who knows in what American album I may be swimming?

Ten years after leaving Iceland we returned for a visit. The warm welcome we received from everyone was repeated at the pool. I smiled at the attendant as I handed in my admission ticket. "I kept this all those years in the States," I said.

The attendant smiled as she pushed the ticket back to me. "We're so happy to see you. I won't take your ticket. Save it to make sure you come back again."

"No, Mrs. Irving, No Brownies!"

"No, Mrs. Irving, no brownies. I cannot let you go outside."

The Marine Sergeant in charge of Embassy Security vetoed my suggestion. When the demonstrators gathered on our street, the sergeant had first made sure the Embassy offices were locked and safe. Then he had come through the connecting door to the Ambassador's Residence to be sure all was in order there.

Suggesting brownies did not mean I was a feather brain about security; but the crowd below our window were college students, and this was Iceland in the 1970s—a country whose police did not carry guns, a country where prison closed for a month each summer to give the guards a vacation; in the fall the prisoners returned to complete their terms. The thirty or so students in front of our home were protesting because the United States was not taking sides (Iceland's) in the current Icelandic-British fishing dispute. They carried a fishing dory, which they put down on the sidewalk. I looked down at the group and thought of my own children in college in the States; I knew that a plate of brownies could relax tension.

"I must ask you to step back from the window so that I can shut the drapes," the Sergeant continued. I was not afraid, but I could picture the page in the Marine Corps Manual that read, "Exposed windows invite rock throwing." The Sergeant was only doing his duty. Should an errant missile strike the Ambassador's wife, his Marine Corps career would be ended. I stepped back and let him close the drapes.

Upstairs I took a discreet peek from the second floor window. The change in the scene below made me smile. In the center of the demonstrators a large empty circle had developed, a circle around the doorstep across the street. Here, in the center of old Reykjavík, as in old villages across New England, doors opened directly onto the sidewalk.

Right now, the door-sill opposite the Embassy was being washed. Frú Gudrún, who lived there on the first floor, had come out to clean her steps—not her usual time of day for this task. Into a pail of sudsy water she dipped her mop, then swished it across the cement, swinging vigorously in all directions. To avoid being soaked the students stepped back. With Icelandic respect for older people, they did not challenge her. This hole in their middle soon led to a dispersal of the crowd, and the group picked up the dory and continued up the street to protest in front of the British Embassy.

As soon as the Marine said it was safe, I fixed a plate of brownies, smaller that the mound I would have taken to the demonstrators and walked across the street to Frú Gudrún's. "We've made some brownies. These are very much liked in the United States." Her smile showed her understanding of my gift. We would both have been embarrassed to say more.

A few months earlier, the Soviets had purchased the building next to Frú Gudrún where there was a photo shop. The location and occupation were a perfect cover for surveillance of our Embassy. We were sure the Soviets tapped our residence telephone. Periodically, U.S. military specialists asked us to leave our home for half a day while they "swept" it for bugs or transmitting devices. Even after such a sweep, if my husband and I had anything secret to discuss, we took a walk. We assumed the walls, like the phones, had ears.

The visit of a good friend, an Ambassador to an iron curtain post, reminded us how common this awareness is in many countries. We had taken him to dinner in Reykjavík's hotel-top restaurant. We were speaking quite openly when his discomfort showed.

"Should you talk that way here?" He asked. We assured him it was all right, but he was not convinced. He lifted the salt, the pepper, and the small flower vase on the table, carefully examining each in turn. "In Bulgaria, we assume all such things hold hearing devices."

We were never afraid in Iceland, but one time we were forced to be given protection. The Bader-Meinhof terrorist gang from Germany threatened to kill an American ambassador stationed in one of the Scandinavian countries. Despite our assurance that Iceland's island geography made it an unlikely choice (how would the foreign assassin escape?), the U.S. insisted Fred have protection around the clock. When

Iceland's President Eldjarn heard of this, he sent the best security team in the country: his own driver and guards. For twenty-four hours a day, in shifts with Icelandic policemen, they sat in our kitchen, rode with Fred in the car to meetings. When we went out in the evening, one sat up front with our driver; two others followed in a second car. One day, much to their joy, the guards on duty joined us in the swimming pool.

After five days, the Bader-Meinhof alert was lifted, and life returned to normal. Fred could travel without a guard, and the President of Iceland had his driver back. Life in Iceland was again safe. I continued to keep a supply of brownies in the freezer.

Little People

When the Department of State sent my husband and me to Iceland, did they know they were getting complementary talents? Did they realize that in this two-for-the-price-of-one couple, they were getting a skilled negotiator to save the NATO Base, and a friend of little people to love Iceland?

Our children know that when I see a circle on the morning grass, I imagine fairies dancing in the night. They know that I smile when I pass toadstools on a rainy day, because I am thinking of small elves hiding under each mushroom umbrella. Our children are sure my link with the little people is part of my Scottish heritage.

In Iceland, the landscape and the long winter darkness combine to encourage thoughts of small unseen creatures. Lava deposits take many forms, whose shadows change with the ever-changing light. Walking through a lava-strewn field in the dark or near dark, or before the arrival of electric lights, people must have welcomed the thought of small friendly folk nearby. In the north of Iceland, where much lava flowed, in an area about the size of two American football fields, is a place called *Dimmuborgir,* shadowy city. It is filled with lava shapes, some over six feet high. When I walked among them it was like walking through a small village.

Often on the farms of Iceland I would see in the corner of a newly mowed field a tuft of uncut grass. "That's where the little people live," explained the first farmer I asked. "If we don't disturb them, they won't disturb us. All creatures have a right to a home." I do not ask him what would happen if the clump were cut. Who would want to find out?

On other farms, there were stories of missing spoons, of pots and pans misplaced, of fires that refused to light, even of illness. When the grass was allowed to grow again, everything returned to normal. The first farmer continued, "I do not say that I know the little people are there. I have never seen them, but how can it hurt to leave that corner unmown? We will never cut it."

Sometimes the small folk live under a rock and sometimes the rock is in the way of a project. In the west of Iceland, a crew putting in a new road reached a point where they kept having problems. One day a wheel would fall off a machine; the next, a gear shift would lock; sometimes the motor wouldn't start; a presumably full oil tank would be without oil; a worker would have such a bad headache, he couldn't work. Finally the crew manager called a halt. He went alone to the rock around which all the problems congregated. The workers watched him standing there a while. On returning, the leader explained, "The little people have their home under that rock. They will move if we wish, but it will take time. If we give them twenty-four hours to do it, they will be gone." The crew understood. They waited the twenty-four hours and then continued the road without mishap. Who is to say why no further problems occurred?

The Icelander who told me the road-building story was a highly educated man who spoke several languages fluently and had been his country's ambassador to several countries. "Do you yourself believe in the little people?" I asked him.

"Dorothy, I only tell you a story that I know happened," he smiled. As I left his home, I noticed in a corner of his city garden a clump of uncut grass.

Pipes and Pumps

My husband and I were not in Iceland in January of 1973 when Heimaey volcano erupted. We had flown home to escort Iceland's Foreign Minister and his wife on an official visit to Washington and to Norfolk's Naval headquarters. Although five more days of consultation were scheduled, as soon as we learned of the eruption, we all knew we had to return to Iceland immediately. It was not a case of knowing what we could do, but simply of knowing that we needed to be there.

Heimaey is located on Iceland's Westmann Island about twenty minutes off the country's south coast. At 1:55 AM on the night of January 23, residents in the town of Heimaey were awakened to police and fire sirens alerting them that the volcano on their island was erupting, shooting forth fire, ash, and stones and pouring lava down its slopes. Police rode through the town with loudspeakers urging people to dress warmly, carry what possessions they could and gather at the harbor for immediate evacuation. Soon a long line of residents was proceeding towards the shore. Behind them under the night sky, they could see the rocks and debris silhouetted against a row of red explosions. In their blood and in their memory, Icelanders are well acquainted with the forces of nature. On the mainland I had visited a recently excavated farm, which had been buried by lava in the Viking days. In the town of Kirkubaerklauster, I had walked on the smooth, hardened surface of old lava, where a nineteenth century flow ended just beyond the town's church while worshippers prayed inside. In recent years the citizens of Heimaey had watched as undersea eruptions of lava created a new island, Surtsey, to their west. Icelanders have seen homes and settlements buried in ash, and seen survivors go on; such people can carry out an island evacuation with equanimity. Without knowing when or if they would return, five thousand islanders boarded boats that night without mishap, confusion, or loss of life. A few remained behind to help save any property they could.

Later, everyone would say how fortunate it was that the severe winds of the previous day had kept Heimaey's fishing trawlers in harbor. The trawlers carrying from forty to four hundred people were soon loaded for the four-hour trip to Thorlakshafn on the mainland's south coast. From that coast, other boats set out towards the island to help. The sea that night was still rough, but the sky was clear for flying. Icelandic and American pilots joined the evacuation effort. The ill and elderly were taken directly to the capital city. One elderly woman, flown from the Westmann Island hospital on a stretcher, smiled at the ambulance crew meeting her in Reykjavík's airport. "I always wanted to see what your hospitals over here are like," she said.

In this national emergency, citizens on the mainland opened their homes to the displaced islanders. Schools, clothes, and housing were found as the entire country helped the evacuees. In Reykjavík it became a joke, that if you saw anyone driving very slowly in the middle of the road it was sure to be a Westmann Islander. "He drives as if he just came over from the Westmann Islands."

In the days after January 23 the eruption continued, threatening the harbor, the life line of that fishing community, and covering ever more of the town with lava and ash. Anything movable that might be buried under that steadily encroaching flow was transported to the mainland. Planes and boats carried refrigerators, household goods, cars, and sheep. One American flyer, a homesick pilot from Iowa, said later, "After three loads of sheep, my plane smelled just like a farm." The vital freezing plant equipment was moved, loaded onto the largest boats. By early March everything salvageable had been taken off the island.

In early March, Icelandic and NATO Base firemen had tried pumping water out of the North Atlantic onto the moving river of lava. They hoped the cooling water would retard the flow enough that the lava might build its own retaining wall. The combined effort of the fireboats and trawlers had little effect, and most observers were ready to agree that this idea would not work. The lava continued moving into the town. In the town, a team of Icelandic workers joined by American seamen from the Base worked around the clock to save or protect whatever buildings they could. They shoveled ash off house roofs, dug away the lava that reached above windows, and cleared paths to doors. But it looked as if the volcano would win.

It was then that a scientist from the University spoke to Sveinn, the Fire Chief of the NATO Base, and the Chief asked to speak to the American Ambassador. Exhausted from hours of trying to control the flames, Sveinn stepped out of his tall fire boots at the door of Fred's office. A strong smell of smoke entered the room with him. He explained the urgency of saving the town and the harbor. This was Iceland's richest fishing village, its economy important to the whole country. The Westmann Islanders hoped to return to their homes. The fishing fleet and the island's freezing plants were their main employers. "Without the harbor," he said, "the town will have no source of income. Without homes, its citizens will have no place to live. The town will die. I want to save it."

"Sveinn, what can I do to help?" Fred asked him.

"There is a young scientist at the University of Iceland who believes that a heavier spraying of water will stop the lava, but we would need a very large number of special pumps and pipes to pull in the water and direct it onto the flow. Our fireboats cannot do it, and the equipment from the NATO Base is not large enough for the job. In the United States there are such special pipes and pumps, no longer in use, I believe. Can you get some for us? In all fairness, I must tell you that a well-known vulcanologist at UNESCO doubts this will work. He says they tried spraying water on an active volcano in Hawaii, and it failed. But that ocean is warm. The scientist believes it will work here because Iceland's water is cold. In my bones, Mr. Ambassador, I believe it will work. We want to try, but we need your help."

Fred looked at Sveinn a moment. This man was an experienced fireman. He had never been untruthful. His instincts were sound, and Fred trusted his judgment. "I'll do what I can, Sveinn. Tell me what you need."

The list was given and what our family called, "the spring of pipes and pumps" began.

First, there was discussion in Parliament. Skeptical members wondered why spend time and money on a project that would probably not succeed. The communist-leaning group in the government did not want to accept help from the United States or from the NATO Base, which they hoped soon to expel. One Cabinet member warned the Foreign Minister that seeking American help might cause his party to leave the coalition government, thus causing the government to fall. He warned that accepting such help could increase public opinion in favor of keeping the Base. When told about this by the Foreign Minister, Fred replied that, in his opinion, if Iceland refused American cooperation, thus letting a community die, it would adversely affect Icelanders' opinion of the government that let it happen, and, most likely, the world's opinion of Iceland. Fred then talked to the Prime Minister who at last spoke for the conscience of his country. "These are our citizens. If there is a chance we can save Heimaey, we must try it."

Fred and the Prime Minister agreed to try to persuade their respective governments to approve joint financing. Fred hoped that the Pentagon and the State Department would see the value of such cooperation not only from a humanitarian point of view but, for the United States, from a military point of view, also.

With the cooperation of the Admiral at the NATO Base, Fred sent a message to U.S. military bases everywhere. He explained the situation and asked them to locate the needed equipment and fly it to Iceland. "This is the equipment we need. What can you supply? How soon can you get it here?" Replies came in to the office and our home several times a day. For three weeks every meal, even breakfast, was interrupted by, "It's a call from Washington, or San Diego, or Norfolk." It came to be an expected part of our mealtime. So expected that when one Sunday dinner was interrupted by a call from our Washington daughter, we spent five minutes exclaiming to her how wonderful it was to have a call from the States that wasn't about pipes and pumps, hose lengths, or delivery days. Finally, she forcefully interrupted our enthusiastic greetings, "Whoa, Mom, Dad, wait a minute. I'm calling to tell you I'm engaged."

Piece by piece, the U.S. Navy rounded up the needed pipes and pumps, and flew them to Iceland on huge cargo planes. Sveinn and his crew set up a long row of pipes and hoses spraying directly onto the river of molten lava, and the constant spraying worked. When the flow of lava was stopped, two thirds of the town still remained; the harbor was lengthened but not closed. "Even improved," said the Westmann Islanders happily.

With the halting of the lava, the phone calls from Washington also slowed. One last message from the Defense Department said it had cost two hundred thousand dollars to transport the equipment, and, although they knew it was important to maintain Iceland's goodwill, they had no money in their multi-billion dollar budget to cover this cost. They would have to bill the American Ambassador personally. When the Ambassador suggested that they dock his salary five dollars a week for eternity, the State Department came to Fred's rescue and paid for the enterprise, meanwhile commenting on the shortsightedness of the Defense Department. U.S. assistance on Heimaey had increased good will in Iceland and helped defuse the feelings of some in the anti-Base group. If the NATO Base were ousted, establishing a less satisfactory base elsewhere would cost the same Defense Department over a billion dollars. One would think two hundred thousand was a bargain.

In May, with lava controlled but still flowing, the first citizens of Heimaey began to move back to the two thirds of their town, which remained unburied. The vast amount of fallen ash was used to lengthen the airport runway and to be the basis of new roads. A simple rubber garden hose lay stretched on the ground carrying the hot underground water to provide heating for the re-opened hospital. With a sense of history and civic pride, Icelanders uncovered the headstones at their town cemetery.

During the months of the eruption, my husband and I had been flown to the island on inspection overflights. In addition, Fred was taken by helicopter for ground level inspections. On one of these he was encouraged to drop a coin into the flowing liquid lava. Later the Fire Chief returned to Heimaey and broke off that now-hardened section. He brought it to the Embassy to give the Ambassador as a token to remember his personal role in the event.

Today that lava, with the coin still visible, rests on the brick colored tile in front of our fireplace. Next to a fire seems an appropriate location for lava, forced out of the earth by heat and flame. When I look at it, I see a tribute to three men: a scientist who was convinced of his idea; a firefighter who had the courage to believe in it, and an ambassador who trusted them both and was able to provide the means they needed. Working together the three men saved a city, a harbor, a community.

ADDENDUM:
Fred's role was remembered.
In 1998, our older daughter, a U.S. government economist, led a study team to Iceland. At their first meeting, her designated Icelandic contact greeted her warmly. "Any daughter of Ambassador Irving is welcome. When Heimaey erupted, your father was the first one who became personally involved in saving the island. We'll never forget him."

Hamrahlid Choir

We heard the songs before we saw the singers. The voices, starting far away, became stronger as they neared our home, filling our city block with music. The chorus from Hamrahlid High School was coming to the Embassy for tea.

My husband and I first heard the group when they sang at one of the biweekly winter concerts of the Reykjavík Symphony Orchestra. In the 1970s people used to say of this orchestra that its playing exemplified "Independent People," the name Iceland's famous author had given his countrymen. But even with many individual and independent interpretations going on, the orchestra was worth hearing. Every other Thursday members of the public, the government, and the diplomatic corps gathered at the Haskolabio for the concerts. The two season's tickets assigned to the American Ambassador were in the center of the hall at the juncture of two aisles, well placed for seeing—and for being seen. When empty, the seats stood out like a gap in a six year old's smile. The position exerted a certain pressure towards regular attendance. We did not miss many Thursdays.

A further inducement to attendance was the use made of intermission, a use of great benefit to government and diplomatic members in the audience. During the break, concertgoers assembled in small groups around the large lobby. Discussions that began with music, could easily—and did often—become occasions for informal, unofficial negotiations, for gentle probing of opinions, for meeting without meeting. On Thursday evenings at the Symphony, one could gather the sense of the community.

The evening the High School Chorus sang, my husband and I were deeply impressed by the beauty of their singing and by the skill, training, and practice it reflected. We sent our thanks to the singers, wrote to the director and invited the group to come to the American Embassy for tea. These were the voices that came singing down our street that Saturday afternoon.

In preparation for the large teenage group, we had filled our long dining room table with sandwiches, brownies, cookies, cakes, soft drinks, coffee, and tea. Missing our own children, now at home in college, we enjoyed conversations with these students. The room held a friendly spirit as we all munched and talked.

After refreshments, the director said the chorus had prepared a short program for us. My husband and I sat in our living room and listened to these young Icelanders sing music of their country and the world. It was possibly the most beautiful concert I have attended. When the students finished they asked if there was any special song we would like to hear. I mentioned my favorite Icelandic lullaby, "*Sofdu, unga astin min,*" "Sleep my darling little one. Outside rain is weeping. Mother holds your treasures safe. We shall not waken during this dark night." The words give a feeling of the long hard winters of isolation and darkness that were once Iceland's. The music, like many of that country's folk songs, is in a minor key. Hearing these young happy voices singing their heritage in my own living room brought tears to my eyes. I could say only, "Thank you," when they finished.

After the group left, we sat silent in appreciation of the pleasure they had given us.

It was not their last gift. Late in December, just at dinner time, we again heard music outside our home. In the cold and dark of winter, it had not come walking down our street; this music came from a bus pulled to a stop outside our door. Each year at Christmas, the Hamrahlid chorus serenades the Reykjavík Old Peoples' Home. Each year their bus makes one stop en route. It might be the home of someone they admire, someone who has served Iceland well, someone they wish to thank. The chorus members meet together and make the choice. This year, their director later told us, the decision had been unanimous. In the cold of that December evening, the Hamrahlid singers stepped out of their bus stood on our sidewalk and sang Christmas carols. They closed with a gentle lullaby of Mary to her Child. Then, even more softly, they added, "*Sofdu, unga astin min.*"

Houseguests

She was the most glamorous houseguest we ever had, and also the most gracious. The glamour was apparent from the moment of her arrival at Keflavik Airport, that Icelandic airport where winds regularly blew thirty miles per hour and up. Winters in Iceland were snowy and blowy. We who lived there wore fitted hats, scarves or kerchiefs against the weather. Umbrellas were useless—inverting or being pulled away by the wind. Mary Travers may have visited Iceland when she wrote that Mary Poppins opened her large umbrella and blew to London. I'm sure it was possible.

Into such an environment, came Mouza Zumwalt, accompanying her husband, Chief of Naval Operations, Admiral Elmo Zumwalt. She stood at the top of the plane's departure stairs looking like a model in her fitted winter coat, small hat, gloved hands holding a parasol. "A parasol?" I gasped silently, but the object deserved no other name. A small ruffled circle held over her head by its slim handle, it would protect her from nothing more than an admiring glance or a very small sprinkle of gentle raindrops. Small sprinkles of gentle rain do not come to Iceland. What would these northern winds do when meeting a parasol, I wondered. Well, they stopped. They rested until she was safely in the limousine at the foot of the plane's steps. The winds, like the rest of us, recognized royalty when it appeared. Mrs. Zumwalt walked down the plane's steps without a hair out of place, protected from all elements by that dainty ruffled circle of cloth.

We drove her to our home, and the Embassy station wagon followed with the trunks. Like "parasol," "trunks" is the surprising but correct word. For a three-day stay, she had brought a queen's wardrobe. Our Embassy guest room, until now adequate if not over-large, seemed too small for someone deserving of a suite. Her graciousness showed at once. "What a lovely room. Thank you very much. I'll rest a little and be down soon."

I went down to the living room. About an hour later, our daughter returning from high school went up to her temporary bedroom in our dressing room; her own bedroom had been given to the Admiral's staff aide. She put down her school books and hurried back to the living room, "Mom, who is that elegant lady swooning in your study?" I went up immediately, to see Mouza, in my desk chair, leaning back, her right hand over her closed eyes, her suede booted legs stretched out in front of her.

"Would it be too much trouble to ask for a cup of tea? I seem to have one of these foolish migraines." She smiled in apology. The tea was immediately brought up.

Later that day she was given a lunch by the navy wives at the Keflavik NATO Base. She sat at the head table interested in everything each person had to say. After lunch, the Base ladies had planned a tour of the new pre-school they had recently developed. To see Mrs. Zumwalt on the tour was to see duty and gallantry in action. She expressed interest in each facet of the school, listened to the difficulties overcome to establish it, and only after a sufficiently long period of time, suggested she might now return to our residence to prepare for her next function. The ladies at the Base never knew of her intense pain. They knew they had shown the wife of the Chief of Naval Operations what they were doing, and she had been interested and admiring of their work. Their lonely base in Iceland was a little less isolated because of her coming.

The important factor was that her interest was sincere. The following day, an Icelander recognized the same sincerity. Knowing of Mrs. Zumwalt's interest in history, I had arranged to take her to Reykjavík's outdoor museum, where houses from periods of Iceland's past are gathered in an outdoor park above the city. It was a museum I loved and visited often. Its director had become a good friend and always welcomed me warmly. I was intrigued that after Mrs. Zumwalt's visit, the director's greeting changed from, "How nice to see you again, Mrs. Irving." to "How is that lovely Mrs. Zumwalt? She was so interested, you know. I always remember her." In a two hour visit Mrs. Zumwalt had left as strong an impression as the one I had developed over three years. But it was merited. Her interest had been so genuine, especially about the early difficult days of Iceland's settlement period. As "White Russians," she and her family had been forced from their home and their country when the communists seized power. She knew life was not always easy. The guide felt the depth of her sympathy and, with it, felt a genuine closeness.

After three days, having charmed the Base, the Embassy and half of Iceland, the Zumwalts left. He had been our houseguest before and we had admired his intelligence, his belief in democratic ideals, his concern for the navy at all its ranks. We now admired him for the strong woman he had chosen as his partner. Of our many high-ranking guests, Admiral Zumwalt was the only one who got out of a car to shake hands with an ordinary citizen neighbor on our Reykjavík street. As he was ready to be driven off in the Ambassadorial limousine one day, my husband told him of the lady across the street who always managed to sweep or wash her front steps whenever any anti-Base demonstration gathered there. "We call her our secret weapon," my husband said. When he heard the story, Admiral Zumwalt asked our driver to wait, went across the street and shook hands with Frú Gúdrun. "Thank you," he said with his wonderful smile, then returned to the car and was driven off to his meeting.

In our four years in Iceland, the Zumwalts were our favorite houseguests. I salute them both.

To Suit The Occasion

It used to be said that the sun never set on the British Empire, and for many years that was true. It was also said—among a smaller group of people—that the sun never set on Swartz's, the clothing company in Maryland. Suits from the Swartz Brothers circled the globe on the backs of American Foreign Service Officers. Measurements of many of those officers were kept on file at the main office of this manufacturer in Baltimore.

Swartz's, known to the Foreign Service as SSS, was a short hour's drive from Washington, D.C., and much of government Washington found its way there. Three brothers had started the firm and had built its success on excellent fabrics, good fitting, and personal service of a highly informal kind. If you were really on their favorite list, you would get taken to the deli next door for a wonderful sandwich and entertaining tales of where and how their suits had fared. (Being a favorite was in no way related to rank or achievement but to something one of the brothers liked about you.)

The first time my husband and I made the trip to Swartz's I was more than a little surprised at what we found. We had been told that the factory-store was in a warehouse, and in a way, that was a compliment to the building. We entered from the parking lot into a huge room, with rows and rows of suits, jackets, and coats, and the three brothers roaming the floor to give advice. A small office on the side was set off by wood part way up the divider and glass on top—much like the newspaper editor offices we see on television. In there, Miss Ellie, their sister, was in charge. She handled accounts and gave advice. Under her leadership, the firm soon developed a line for women which became as successful as was the men's line. The year the firm offered a sleeveless wool shell and matching full length coat, I bought three to take along to Vienna—one in yellow, one in white, and one in rose. Soon all of my suits were from Swartz's, and even now, twenty years out of the service, I still have two of them. They never wear out.

In a large room off to the right the cutters and tailors worked at long tables. Here, too, were the rolls of fabric. If you wanted a suit in a fabric you did not see, you could be taken back there to pick from the very fine materials on hand. If you wanted part of a suit reshaped it was no problem to the tailors, provided only that one of the brothers or one of the longtime senior salesmen approved of the line you wanted. If not, the brother or senior salesman would remind you that it would really look awful that way, and that you really didn't want to do it. When that happened, the customer usually found it easier to change his mind.

When our son was ready for his first full suit we took him to Swartz's, a trip he may not recall with complete pleasure. While standing on the platform to have the length measured, the teenager kept lowering his pants to where he usually wore them. Brother Louis came over. "No, no," he said. "You wear your pants here, not there," as he hoisted the trousers some inches upwards. If said softly, this advice would have been no problem, but it was declared in a ringing voice to the tailor and to anyone else in that half of the large warehouse.

"Look how he's wearing his pants!" Louis shouted. Rick has never forgotten it.

On trips to Swartz's we always met at least one other Washington-based family. Shoppers came from all ranks of government and from other professions where the word had spread. We went there over a period of thirty years for any of our needs in the line of suits or coats—and always before an overseas tour.

The most dramatic story our family has from SSS is the story of the Ambassador's tuxedo, an event that occurred when my husband was U.S. Ambassador to Iceland. We had just received an alert that President Nixon and President Pompidou of France would be holding a meeting in Iceland, and that President Nixon would be staying at our residence. Of course, with such an historic meeting between two presidents, there would be many functions, both formal and informal. In checking out clothes before the visit, my husband found a sizable tear in his tuxedo jacket. It would never see him through the events ahead. With alarm, he phoned Baltimore and Swartz's. The brother on the phone assured him that they would quickly make a duplicate jacket (my husband's measurements were among those on file), and they would get it to him in Iceland in time for the visit five days later. They did make it, it did fit, and it did arrive on time. It was the mode of transport that gave the story its dramatic tinge. Allowing time to make the jacket, the only way to get it to post would be by a direct flight, and the ideal flight on that given day was the President's plane bringing Nixon to Iceland for his meeting with Pompidou. As the President stepped out of the front door of Air Force One, a package for the Embassy was handed out the cargo door. It was the tuxedo jacket. We often said we had the classiest delivery service in the world. Who else had the President of the United States deliver a suit?

The tuxedo delivery was the second time the Swartz brothers had come quickly to our aid. Many years earlier at dinner on a trip to Kenya, my husband had spilled some sauce on the trousers of his best State Department Blue suit. "State Department Blue" was a term all American diplomats recognized. It meant a plain dark suit, either summer or winter weight, suitable for all occasions that were important but not formal. Such a suit was appropriate and necessary for a range of events: official calls on government offices, State Funerals, National Day observances: Bastille Day, Independence days and such. When it became clear that the Kenya stain was permanent, my husband wrote to the brothers Swartz, asking them to make a new pair of trousers for the suit he had recently bought there. When he arrived back in Washington two weeks later, the replacement trousers had been made and delivered to our home. No wonder these men were loved!

My own special memory of an SSS outfit comes from the day I represented the United States at National Day in Iceland. On that day, June 17, heads of diplomatic missions and their wives meet in the old Icelandic Parliament building, march across the street to the National Church, and then proceed in ranking order to the city square for official ceremonies. They walk between a double row of Icelandic flags held by uniformed Icelandic Boy and Girl Scouts. On our third 17th of June in Iceland, my husband awakened very ill. He immediately phoned the Secretary General of the Foreign Office to say he would be unable to attend National Day and would ask his deputy to represent the American Embassy. The Secretary General said, "Wait," paused a moment, and then asked, "Couldn't Dorothy represent the United States by herself? We'd like to have her." Of course, I could, and how proudly I did. Our place in diplomatic rank (established by the date of one's arrival in the country) was after the Swedish and before the Norwegians. So, as these diplomatic couples proceeded across the town square, behind the Swedish Ambassador and his wife, and in front of the Norwegian pair, a woman walked alone representing the United States. In my SSS white wool dress and rose princess style coat, I walked as tall as I ever had. Miss Ellie and the brothers would have been proud.

Foreign Service Pets

The Icelandic State Veterinarian made an appointment to call at the home of the American Ambassador. "I'll be there Monday at four," he said. "Until then the creature must be kept in a cage and all papers must be kept with it."

The creature was Hal, our younger daughter's pet rabbit, and his papers were numerous. When our son, Rick, strode from the plane early Monday morning, we could not tell if the cage he carried held a rabbit or not. The sides of it were completely covered with affidavits tied onto the wire mesh. Sealed in plastic were certificates of health from town and from state, certificate of ownership, certificate of absence of rabies, of absence of hoof and mouth disease, permission to fly in the passenger cabin of the plane. Barbara lifted the largest piece of laminate, "Hi, Hal."

"Heavens," I asked Rick when I saw all the legal forms. "Did you have any trouble getting these?"

"No problem," said our college junior. "The vet was very understanding. He said he sends a lot of animals overseas. But I wish you'd been there when I checked in at Kennedy Airport. I put Hal's case on the conveyor belt, and while I walked through the metal detectors I heard a loud shriek, 'There's a rabbit in there! Hey, look. It's alive. It's a real rabbit. Look.'" It was the attendant monitoring the x-ray screen.

"Were you embarrassed?" I laughed.

"No, I just put on my best 'what usually comes-through-airport-conveyor belts?' expression, and acted very nonchalant as I picked him up." Rick is good at nonchalance.

When we had moved to Iceland in October of Barbara's senior high school year, we did not expect to have Hal follow us. During our four years in Washington, Barbara and Rick had raised a series of rabbits on the screened porch of our suburban home. Our favorites were Hal, the first of them, and Mushroom, that dedicated mother who pulled out her own fur to make a warm nest for each new litter. When Rick went to college, he gave away his half of the rabbits, and just before leaving the States, Barbara had found homes for the others. Only Hal was kept. Barbara left him with a friend and promised to come back and visit him.

Our assignment to Iceland was our first overseas tour with only one child. Our older two were now at home in college and graduate school. Barbara had to finish her senior year at the NATO Base high school at Keflavík, a long bus ride each day to a school she did not like. After a few months my husband and I realized how much she missed her siblings, her friends, her old school—none of which we could transport to Iceland. We asked for permission to import Hal. Hal had gone to summer camp with Barbara; surely he could travel across the Atlantic. Rick said he would bring the rabbit on his next college vacation, and now Hal was here. Barbara was delighted and we all felt a sense of accomplishment. We had finally brought a pet overseas, small though he was.

This was not the first time we had tried to take a pet abroad. Fifteen years earlier, when we were assigned to New Zealand, we wanted to take our much-loved schnauzer, Thor. We knew Foreign Service families who had successfully taken pets to Europe. While the family crossed the ocean in a stateroom, the dog or cat was up on the kennel deck, where the family could visit whenever they wished.

But New Zealand, like Iceland, is an island country and can easily protect its borders from rabies, hoof and mouth, and other diseases. For Thor to move from Washington to Wellington, he would have been sent to England for six months of quarantine, and then shipped out—across the Atlantic and the Pacific—to us in New Zealand. During the six months in London, the dog would see no familiar face and hear no familiar voice. The courteous man explaining the rules said we were, of course, most welcome to visit our pet at any time. The trip from New Zealand to Great Britain seemed a long and expensive journey to pat a furry head no matter how much loved. We couldn't do it and we were not sure how a twelve-year-old dog would survive the long separation.

We looked for a family who would want him. After several interviews the choice was clear. A mother, father and two children came to our home to meet the dog. While we talked, the father sat in the arm chair by the fireplace and soon Thor came out of his favorite spot under the piano and sat next to him—a most unusual performance. Thor had chosen his new family. A few days later the family picked him up. Our farewell view was of two children in the back seat with the dog between them. Thor did not look back, and soon I couldn't continue looking. Although the family invited us to see Thor in his new home, we declined. One goodbye was enough for both sides of this friendship. The family wrote us when he died.

Parting with Thor had been so hard, we considered not having another pet. But on our next tour home we succumbed and once again acquired a schnauzer. We named him Thor ll. This dog was never a candidate for overseas life. He was the only dog in his class to fail obedience school. Also—there is no gentle or polite way to say it— sometimes Thor II bit. Whenever he got out of the house unleashed, family members would rush out front and side doors to find him before any damage was done. Thor bit other dogs, a few cats, a hen, a duck, and, much to the embarrassment of our high school daughter, two boyfriends. One boy made the mistake of reaching too quickly for a potato chip in a bowl on the coffee table; the second, helping us decorate our Christmas tree, reached too hastily to pick up an ornament on the floor. At ten on Christmas Eve we took the boy to the hospital emergency room for stitches. We did not see how we could take such a dog overseas. We did not think he would help us to win friends abroad. We learned of a family who lived out in the country, who wanted a dog with strong spirit and a strong sense of family (Thor never bit any of *us*). When they and Thor met, all seemed happy together. He lived with them a long time.

But now, on this Monday morning in Iceland, our first overseas pet had arrived. Once home from the airport, we found that by clipping those affidavits together with clothespins above Hal's cage he could see out and we in. We dared not remove a single paper until the vet arrived.

At four o'clock the doorbell rang. The official examined the rabbit and then spoke to Barbara with great seriousness, "You must NEVER let him run loose outside; if he is ever sick you or your parents must call me immediately. We will see that he is destroyed."

I smiled politely, made no comment.

"Do you understand?" He asked of us and of Barbara.

"Yes, I do," she answered. Permission was granted for the rabbit to remain, and the visit was completed with a friendly glass of sherry.

As soon as the man left, we rejoiced and let Hal out of his cage. He had made it. We had brought a pet overseas. We saluted both absent Thors. My husband built a rabbit run on the long sunny landing across the back stairs of the Residence. Remembering that Rick and Barbara had once built a cage in our Maryland basement and then found it too large to get up the stairs, my husband constructed his in place. Here Hal stayed until Barbara also went home to college. Hal moved out briefly during President Nixon's stay in the house. A corner of an unused office in the Embassy was found for his cage, and with a special security pass to enter the building, Barbara went there each day to feed and see her rabbit. The President was amused when he learned about the arrangements.

Hal would surely have some stories to tell if we let him.

Roundup

I pulled my brown Icelandic sweater over my head, pulled up my brown slacks, stepped into my loafers, and went down to the car. We had told our Embassy driver we wanted to see a sheep roundup; he had located one about an hour's drive outside of Reykjavík.

In mid September, all over Iceland farmers round up their sheep and their horses. The animals, released into the hills to graze for the summer, now, before winter, are brought back to their farms. A roundup may take from a day to a week; meadow areas in the mountains are large, and farmers go both on foot and on horseback to herd their animals down towards the gathering pens. At Skagafjjord in north Iceland, forty men brought in over three thousand sheep and more than two hundred horses.

The roundup we would visit was a smaller one, perhaps a thousand sheep. I was looking forward to it. The day was beautiful, cool and crisp; pale blue sky spread as far as we could see. The wind, which could be so strong, was gentle today. I did not need my warm Icelandic ear-covering hat.

We drove into the countryside past fields of moss-covered lava. A few moss flowers in red and yellow still bloomed. Our gravel road followed the shore of a small lake, and as the car turned the last bend I saw the roundup ahead of us. About twenty cars and trucks were gathered around a large circular pen. The trucks were the large farm ones with slatted sides. Several backed up to the pen's outer fence; others were parked off to the side. On the hillside beyond, boys on horseback, helped by lively black and white farm dogs were holding the already gathered sheep in a large group. In the distance, more dogs and horses urged lagging sheep down from the hills. On the left as we parked a woman was handing out food to three small children. On the far side of the pen two boys about eight were playing tag with three girls on a low hill. Women talked together in small groups. Most of the men and larger boys stood in clumps around the gathering pen.

I climbed up on the wood fence at the edge of the pen's round enclosed area. The center was empty and an outer rim was divided into several narrow wedges. It was the shape of an angel cake for a giant. (Icelandic folk tales often mention giants.) Each outer section had two gates, one opening into the center gathering area and a second, which opened to the back of a parked truck.

Even before the sheep entered the center pen, I could feel excitement in the air and also a sense of continuing history. For a thousand years, Icelanders had been rounding up their sheep in this fashion. At one time, Iceland's annual parliamentary meeting outdoors in June had been a time of gathering for the whole country, an occasion when the whole nation came together for a week on the Plains of Parliament. With the growth of Reykjavík and the erection of a parliament building there, this custom had ended; Parliament Plains were now historic, used only for ceremonial occasions. But the smaller gatherings of the sheep roundup still occurred. All over Iceland, these gatherings of local families were taking place—an outing for a day or two, a chance to see all the neighbors from farms in the area, a catching up of news and friendships. A community event, not put on for fun, but part of the year round need of the farms and the people who lived on them. I felt one with the country.

As the farm boys opened the gate, the sheep pushed into the center pen. Black, brown (one was the exact color of my sweater), white, creamy, mixed, they jostled together. The smell of wool and of sheep arose. Baa-ing of the crowded sheep became very loud. You could not talk over it. When the center was full, two boys closed the gate. Young and old farmers pushed into the crowded pen to find their sheep. I had been told each sheep was marked, but no farmer needed to look for the identification. Each man and boy recognized the animals from his own home farm. "Well, Bessi, have a good summer? Here we go. How that young one's grown!" "Come along, Gizur, into the pen. Still stubborn, I see." Each farmer straddled his sheep as he found it, led it by ears or horns until he could push it into his own outer wedge, then went back to find another. When the inner circle thinned out, more of the waiting herd were let inside. I was not the only one standing on the rail watching. Boys and girls, farmers not in the pens, young children who called to their fathers, *"Sjádu, Pabbi, Stulka. Sjádu."* "Look, Daddy Stulka. Look!" I may have been the only woman on the fence, but I really did not notice. Women who came every year may have been more interested in seeing friends, than in watching the sheep. But I had never been to a roundup. I was there, and I needed to see what happened. We stayed for about two hours.

Then I reluctantly climbed down for the drive home. We were having dinner at the French Ambassador's that evening, and I would need to shower away the sheep smell, put on a long dress, and look official.

It is no reflection on the French Ambassador that I do not remember his dinner. When I remember Fall in Iceland, I think of horses and sheep coming down from the mountains and the breeze in my hair as I once stood on a fence rail and watched. And, sometimes, when I cut wedges from an angel cake, I remember the roundup.

City Hospital

Thórunn, Hjördís, Gudrún, Jóhanna, Erna, Helga, Hrafnhildur, Áslaug, Dorothy. The schedule for Red Cross volunteers was on the bulletin board at Reykjavík's City Hospital. I smiled to see Dorothy in that sea of Icelandic names.

The days of the week listed when volunteers would be staffing the hospital library and going on the floors with the book cart. Manudagur (Monday) headed the column with my name. I was assigned to wing B/E-6.

Two friends, Thórunn and Gudrún, had invited me to join the Red Cross and work with them at the hospital. I expressed concern about my still limited Icelandic. "Supposing someone who is ill cannot understand me. It doesn't seem right to upset someone who is hospitalized." "Oh, your Icelandic is so good now," they urged, "and you already know many of the other women doing this." "We'll be there to guide you the first few days."

Always eager for expanded contact with Iceland, I went with them the following Monday. Thórunn introduced me to the Director of Volunteers, who seemed genuinely pleased if a little surprised at my joining the group. She showed me the dressing room where the volunteers' blue smocks hung. Each smock had a hospital crest and most carried metal name tag pins. I saw Thórunn's name and others I recognized. "Take any jacket without a name." The director described the duties. "You get your cart at the library when you come, fill it with or add books and set out for your assigned floor. Long-time patients may have books to return." She explained how this was done. "For patients to sign out a book use a blue card. You will find the patients very glad to see you. We usually go on the floors two at a time."

I was glad of the two at a time custom. The day I started neither of my friends was assigned to my floor. "You'll be fine," assured Gudrún. "Áslaug will be there. She knows you're coming. She will help you." I met Áslaug in the dressing room and indeed she was helpful and friendly as we pulled on our jackets, hers with a bona fide metal name pin, mine with a paper sticker reading, "Dorothy." We found our cart at the library and took it to the third floor. "Oh," Áslaug exclaimed. "I need more cards. I'll be right back. Just wait right here." I was happy to "wait right here." As a library assistant who spoke a limited amount of Icelandic, surrounded by rooms of ill people who probably spoke no other language, I wasn't eager to wander around on my own.

A patient in a blue hospital robe approached the cart carrying a book. "I've finished this," she said in Icelandic. "Do you have any other mysteries?" Áslaug had shown me how the cart was arranged. I pointed the patient to the mysteries on the middle shelf. "Have you read this?" she asked, lifting out a book. Had I read an Icelandic mystery? Hardly. "No, but I see it's been checked out frequently. It must be a book many have liked." She signed it out, and I looked around for my still absent co-worker. After two more visits from ambulatory patients, I dared to enter a bedroom. The sunny two-bed room was inviting and both patients looked up as I came in. *"Godan Dayan,"* I greeted. Both women smiled. I wheeled the cart between their beds, asked how they were feeling, and showed them some books. Each chose a book and thanked me. Feeling very successful at leaving two books behind, I returned to the hallway to see Áslaug waiting and smiling. Why did I think that she had purposely left me on my own to sink or swim?

"Er tu vesternislandur?" "Are you a Western Icelander?" they asked in the next room. "Western Icelander" referred to Icelandic citizens who had emigrated to Canada or the United States. Even though they used English in their daily life, such people aggressively clung to their own language. They taught it to their children; they published Icelandic language newspapers, and continued the celebration of Icelandic holidays and customs. Over many years such emigrants had begun to speak Icelandic with a slight American or Canadian accent. This was where many Icelanders placed me. "No, I am an American," I always answered. "But you speak Icelandic so well." "Thank you. It's a beautiful language."

And so it happened that every Monday afternoon I was at Reykjavík's

City Hospital, working with friends new and old, and meeting ever more of the populace of Iceland. Perhaps my most surprising encounter was on my third Monday. I entered a room where a patient was recovering from a heart attack. She was frightened and discouraged about what the future might hold for her, about what she might still be able to do in life. Hoping it was the right thing, and hoping my Icelandic words would be accurate, I reassured her based on my own experience. "Several years ago, I, too, had a heart attack," I told her. "I remember worrying about what it would mean for my future. I recovered slowly, but I am now well and can do everything I want. Except," I smiled, "I still do not lift heavy parcels. I hope you will be well, too. I was frightened at first, but, as you can see, I am fine now." She seemed encouraged. The following week she had gone home.

That same day the Foreign Minister's wife was in the hospital visiting a friend. "Dorothy," she said as she saw me in the hall, "I didn't know you did this, too. How nice. Come with me and meet my old school friend." The next Monday, another political contact seemed surprised to see me in my blue jacket. The leader of a political party, a man often quite outspoken against the United States, he glanced unseeingly at yet another lady in blue, then looked again. "Mrs. Irving, do you work with the Red Cross?"

"Yes, every Monday I am here," I smiled. "Do you have someone ill?" "My mother has just had surgery. I didn't expect to see you here." "I hope your mother is doing well. Oh, excuse me," another patient had approached my cart needing help.

I told my husband about the encounter. The following day my husband saw the same politician at a meeting "He was much friendlier than I have ever seen him. Did you wave a magic wand over him?"

So often, things I did in Iceland because of my own interest proved to be of benefit to the Embassy. Our second day in Iceland we had asked to go to Thingvellir, the location on the plains where Iceland's parliament used to hold its annual outdoor meetings. We did not then know this was the heart of Iceland, nor did we immediately know how pleased Icelandic members of our Embassy were by our early visit there. My first week in Iceland I applied for a library card, not thinking of the favorable impression this would make in this most literate of countries. I read *Landnamabok,* the book of the settlements, the book that records who settled where and who were the descendants of those first settlers. Every Icelander knows it by heart. Before leaving Washington, I had read *Njal's Saga,* the most famous and most beloved of Iceland's sagas. Things I liked were things Icelanders valued. Iceland and I were a good match.

I had been at the City Hospital a few weeks when the Director verified with me the spelling of Dorothy. She wanted to order an official hospital pin for me to wear on rounds. I was surprised at how disappointed I was that we were transferred before I could receive and wear my pin. Perhaps my level of disappointment was so great because it told me that no matter how much we love or take part in another country, we are never really a member of it; we stop just short of really belonging—and so we should. Still, I would have been proud to have a City Hospital pin reading "Dorothy." I would have brought it home.

Diplomatic Cable

"Are the apple blossoms in bloom in Hardanger?" The American Ambassador's cable to the Norwegian Foreign Office was not classified; everyone in the Embassy (and who knows where else) could read it.

"The apple blossoms?" the Political officer asked the Economic Officer. "What do you suppose it means? The old man hasn't mentioned any problems with Norway."

The Deputy Ambassador went across the hall to see his boss.

"Sir, I just read the morning cables. Is there anything I should be doing? Can I be of help?"

The junior consular officers, on their first tour overseas, and eager for intrigue, pondered together. "It has to be a code," they decided, "written, no doubt, to confuse those electronic devices the Soviets are always aiming at us. Wonder what's up."

The Ambassador's secretary, close mouthed as always, shrugged her shoulders when officers hinted for an answer as to what was going on.

Although concern was lessened because those who knew him could see no change in the Ambassador's demeanor—he was as calm as this man ever was—there was extra alertness in the Embassy staff. Their antennae were out, seeking any nuances of speech or behavior in the Embassy or in the community, any detail that might have significance later when the wire was understood.

Two days later the return cable came in. The Communications clerk carried it to the Ambassador's secretary.

"I think he's waiting for this." The clerk handed the printout across the desk.

"I'll take it right in."

"Apple blossoms should reach their peak, week of May 17th. Regards, Olaf."

Norway's Ambassador to Iceland, now on vacation in Oslo, had answered Fred's cable. Olaf had always said that the best time to visit Hardanger Fjord was in apple blossom season. The Norwegian envoy had looked up the expected dates of this year's bloom, delighted at the thought that his friend and colleague's vacation would be scheduled to see Norway at its springtime best.

Diplomatic Language

Diplomatic language is sometimes formal: "Your Excellency, I have the honor to inform you ..." or, "My government regrets that it is necessary to..." Sometimes the words of diplomacy are day-to-day language in seemingly day-to-day situations. Speaker Tip O'Neill used to say all politics is local. My husband and I believed that the best diplomacy is personal.

During our tour in New Zealand, Fred and I had become close friends with a member of the opposition political party, a party frequently in disagreement with U.S. policy. As a member of the Foreign Relations Committee in Parliament, our friend gave many speeches on international relations. One evening he phoned to alert us that the following day in Parliament he would have to give an anti-American speech. He wanted us to know that this speech was for local political reasons and we shouldn't believe it represented his personal views. I could hear only my husband's half of the conversation.

"Really, Joseph, do you have to? That's too bad." And then, "Joseph, I can hardly hear you. What did you say?" "Joseph, I do believe you're getting laryngitis. How do you feel?" The next day's parliamentary report cited that an opposition leader had been unable to make his expected anti-American speech because of a severe attack of laryngitis.

In another country we received a phone call asking, "Dorothy, if you're taking your usual walk this morning why don't you stop in for coffee?" The Prime Minister's wife, who had become a close friend, issued the neighborly invitation. This was at a tense time in negotiations about retention of the NATO Base in her country. Fred and I sensed that a significant anti-Base action was in the air, but we couldn't define the timing of the threat. My morning coffee gave us the answer. The Prime Minister's wife, a devoted patriot of her own land, and a friend of ours, was knowledgeable about government affairs, as she knew I was. When I left her home that day, she said, "Dorothy, I think it would be good if Fred called my husband this afternoon." The message had been the reason for my invitation. Fred did call, and the two men worked together to prevent an action that would have undermined the sensitive base negotiations. Had they waited another day it would have been too late.

Diplomatic language also educated us as to where to find good Chinese food. When two countries do not recognize each other, their diplomats at a post have no interchange, either formally or informally. Such was the case with us and the Chinese in Iceland. We did not mind the lack of conversation, but we kept hearing from our colleagues—from countries that did recognize China—about the wonderful meals they had at that Embassy. We both love Chinese food. Our third year in Iceland, the Chinese Ambassador became Dean of the Diplomatic Corps, a position that goes to the incumbent ambassador who has been longest at the post. It is sort of a Gold Cane of Diplomacy. As Dean, he had to host certain functions, which included all members of the Corps, even us. At one such function, my husband decided to tease him a little. "My wife and I love Chinese food," he said, knowing full well no invitation would be forthcoming, "Where is a good place to get some?" With a perfectly straight face, the Chinese Ambassador in Reykjavík, Iceland replied that there are some very good Chinese restaurants in New York City.

And then, there is diplomatic sign language. In Iceland our home was adjacent to the Embassy office building, with a connecting door on the second floor. Senior diplomats know in the back of their minds that they are on duty twenty-four hours a day. With this connected living arrangement, such knowledge was in the front of our minds. I sometimes wondered if people living upstairs over a store shared this feeling. For nighttime emergency messages, the proximity was convenient. One Saturday morning my husband received a 4:00 AM call from the U.S. Marine on duty in the Embassy. There was a message he needed to see. Dressing quickly he went across to his office. I was still comfortably in bed when he returned.

"Emergency?" I asked sleepily.

"Company," he replied.

"Staying here?"

A nod.

"Soon?"

Another nod.

"Someone special?"

A serious nod.

I began to wake up. "A Senator?"

My husband's hand pointed upwards. Even in our beloved Iceland, there were some things we did not say out loud in our home; the Soviets often had receivers trained on the house.

My mouth shaped the words, "The Secretary of State?"

My husband shook his head, the finger still pointing to the ceiling.

"The Vice-President?"

The head still said no; the finger still pointed up

"The President?" My brain started scrambling through arrangements.

"When?" It was our first word of the Nixon-Pompidou summit to be held in Reykjavík three weeks later.

And, finally, a diplomatic conversation with one who made no pretense of being a diplomat. My husband and I were home alone when the doorbell rang about nine-thirty one evening. The front door at street level was one flight below the living room where we sat. I went to the intercom to ask who was there. The conversation was in Icelandic.

"Hello. May I help you?"

"Is this the American Embassy?"

"Yes, it is."

"I have to see the Ambassador right away."

"What is your name?" *(Hvad heitur pu?)*

He gave his name. "I have to come in and see the Ambassador."

I thought that letting in is easier than putting out. "He's very busy just now. Why do you have to see him?"

"I have to come in and kill him."

"What did you say?" Had my budding Icelandic failed me?

"I have to come in and kill him." There had been no error on my part.

"You can't do that tonight. He's very busy."

"I can't leave until I do it."

"Perhaps you could come back another time."

"When?"

"Come back tomorrow when the Embassy is open." The Embassy's Marine guards would be better interference than I.

"All right. I'll do that. What time does the Embassy open?"

"It opens at nine in the morning."

"I'll be back then."

"Good night."

"Good night."

He left, and amazement covered our faces. We were about to call the police when the phone rang.

"Sir, we wanted you to know not to worry. That man who was ringing your doorbell, we have taken him into custody and returned him to the mental hospital. He escaped earlier this evening, and we followed him to your home. We were outside the whole time he was talking, but we thought Mrs. Irving was handling it so well, and her Icelandic was so good, we just stayed there and listened until they were through. Have a good night, sir."

President Nixon's Visit

In 1973, the first week in May, the Embassy received a telegram that in three weeks President Nixon and President Pompidou of France would hold a summit meeting in Reykjavík. The second week in May, an Air Force plane arrived, bringing the eight member White House advance team. They came to survey the city and to plan the logistics of the visit: to see where meetings might be held, where the accompanying US officials might stay, to decide where the President should stay. They considered space, security, and availability of communications.

Their two day visit was a whirlwind of activity. The team looked at Reykjavík's hotels, they visited the city's new art museum with its large public spaces, and they toured the Ambassador's Residence. On the Residence visit I asked an aide who was going upstairs to our second floor if I couldn't hold his briefcase for him. No thanks, he said, he could carry it. With a start I realized my newness to this game. His briefcase held the White House communications code. It never left the aide's hand.

The team chose the large art museum as the place for the meetings. They made reservations at the largest hotel for members of the Cabinet and White House staff who would be accompanying the President. Then they were ready to decide where President Nixon would stay.

The Marine Major in charge of the team asked to meet with my husband and me. He sat opposite us in the den off the living room. "We're concerned that the Soviets own the building across the street and that it houses a photo studio, but despite that we think the President would be most comfortable here at the Residence."

We thought so, too.

The Ambassador's Residence in Iceland was smaller than those in Rome, London, or Oslo. In Oslo, the house was so large, the

Ambassador and his wife had connected telephones to their children's bedrooms, and established an in-house system of call bells. In such a home visitors could easily co-abide with a family. In Iceland there were three and a half bedrooms, three baths and an office upstairs, plus the public rooms down stairs. There was no way that two families could be apart from each other.

"Because the residence is small," the Major continued, "would you and your family be willing to live somewhere else during the President's stay? And your staff will have to be given time off. The President always travels with his own cook and valet." We knew all world leaders carry their own food and water. Indeed, many years ago, a Hindu leader had carried drinking water from India to Great Britain.

The White House team seemed surprised at our willing acceptance. "Usually," they said, "the Ambassador—well, often the Ambassador's wife—feels a presidential visit is a nuisance." They were surprised again later when our high school daughter happily helped deliver information packets to the hotel rooms for the expected arrivals. For her it was being part of history.

Once all decisions were made, the Major met with my husband and me to review responsibilities for each facet of the visit.

"We'll need a Control Officer for the Residence, someone to be sure everything is in readiness here."

"I think I would be the best person for that," I offered.

"We have never had a wife do it."

"Well, I am the one who best knows the house. I will see that everything is done." He looked at me a moment, then accepted.

I asked, "Is there anything you can suggest now that would make things more comfortable for the President? Anything that is needed here at the Residence?"

"He likes to sit with his feet up. You may have read in the papers about the phlebitis in his legs. He enjoys Lawrence Welk recordings. Also," this was said politely, if firmly, "that desk in the study should be cleaned off in case the President wants to use it." It was my always full desk he described.

"Fine," I replied.

The advance team returned to Washington, and we in Reykjavík started on our preparations. There was no hassock for the presidential feet, but a reliable helper at the Embassy found leftover material that matched an easy chair in the first floor den, and he found an upholstery shop that would build and cover a large hassock in a week. We sent out an Embassy-wide message asking to borrow Lawrence Welk records. There were frequent conversations with Washington and each request was taken care of. I cleaned off my desk. The American and French Embassies found hotel rooms for the expected six hundred press of their two countries.

I surveyed the Residence as a whole. Whenever President Eisenhower visited an embassy, word went ahead that his wife liked to sleep in a pink bedroom. For many years in several capitals of the world, there were "Mamie-pink" bedrooms, freshly painted for a presidential visit. President Nixon's team told us this president did not want to arrive to the smell of fresh paint. Instead we wiped and cleaned the walls. The head of Reykjavík's largest hotel came to the door the morning I was scrubbing fingerprints off woodwork in the entry.

"I didn't know Ambassadors' wives scrubbed walls," he said.

"Erik," I answered, "Ambassadors' wives do whatever needs doing." I knew mine was the best eagle eye in the Embassy to find any marks on woodwork. In truth, I scrub woodwork wherever I live. That same morning, after the carpet cleaners said they did only floors, and the window cleaners said they didn't do walls, I had been the one to wipe fingerprints off the wall behind my husband's office desk.

To prepare our home for President Nixon's stay we faced one more task: checking all rooms for items that showed our family had supported this man's opponent in the last election. A Career Foreign Service Officer is by definition non-partisan and is expected to carry out all duties in a non-partisan manner. Although my husband and I could not take part in partisan political activities, our children could, and often did. On a final check the day before the President's arrival, we turned over a pencil holder in Barbara's room and a "Humphrey for President" pin fell out. We removed all these things not to act a lie, but to prevent any upset to a man who should be at his most alert in negotiations with the leader of another country.

Late the third week in May, crews flew in from the States bringing food and electrical equipment. With them came a security team to make a final check of the house. The food team stored and labeled the food. The electricians wired the Residence for instant communication with Washington. When they finished, one phone in each room connected directly to the White House switchboard. Our high school senior, missing friends and classmates in Washington, was greatly tempted by the thought of free phone calls home. All she need do when someone answered, was to give a friend's phone number. She picked up the phone to see what would happen. When she heard the polite words, "White House Switchboard. May I help you?" she answered quickly, "No, thank you," and put down the receiver.

Meanwhile, the security team swept through the house. They lifted furniture cushions, shook out curtains, went through all closets and drawers. In our study they handed my husband a piece of paper, a note that opened, "Dear Dick."

"Your letter to the President was wedged behind a desk drawer," they said. "We knew you'd want it."

"Thank you." was the only possible answer. Neither of us smiled. We did smile later when we forwarded the letter to our college friend, Dick, and told him the story.

Late in May, we faced the challenge of assigning cars. The President would have his own limousine, flown out from Washington a day ahead to be waiting at the airport when he landed. Our Embassy reserved rental cars for the officials who would be accompanying him. Four days before everyone would arrive, my husband received two requests for the use of his Ambassadorial limousine. The State Department asked that he make it available for use by Secretary of State Rogers; forty-five minutes later, the National Security Council phoned to request its use for Henry Kissinger, then head of NSC. We faced these two competing egos wanting the same car. My husband's reply (a true one) was that the official car was "unreliable." The Public Affairs Officer of the Embassy came to the rescue. He was friendly with the local head of Coca Cola, an Icelander who had two identical new Lincolns and was happy to make them available, one for the Secretary of State and one for the head of the National Security Council. A personality clash was averted.

During the discussion of cars, Ottó, our Embassy driver, asked my husband, "Mr. Ambassador, since you are the personal representative of the President, does that mean that during the three days he is here you are really no one?" "Yes, Ottó," my husband replied, "that is true, but you may want to remember that there are 362 other days in the year, and that next year will have 365 days." Always quick to determine on which side his bread was buttered, Ottó answered with a crisp, "Yes, Sir." He accepted the concept so completely that during the visit, when asked to drive Rosemary Woods, the President's secretary, somewhere, he came to me and asked if it was all right. "I really work for you and the Ambassador, not Miss Woods," he said. "Ottó, thank you, but the best thing you can do for us is to make sure Miss Woods has a good experience here in Reykjavík." Later, I saw Rosemary Woods freeze when Dan Rather entered the Icelandic wool shop where I took her shopping. I was glad a reluctant driver wasn't upsetting her further.

The day of the visit finally came. Our clean—in every sense—Residence was ready. For security reasons, the street was closed to traffic; our family car had a special decal so that our daughter could drive into our street to feed her rabbit, temporarily moved from the Residence to an empty office in the Embassy.

My husband greeted Air Force One when it arrived at Keflavík Airport. Then he returned to Reykjavík to stand at the door of the Residence with Barbara and me. An FBI agent stood by our side. We could overhear his constant communication with the President's motorcade. He alerted us when it was about to enter our street. My husband and I were accustomed to riding in an official limousine with a flag flying on each front fender, the American flag on the right, and the Ambassadorial flag on the left. We were accustomed to seeing similar limousines carrying ambassadors and flags of other nations. So I was not prepared for the excitement I felt when the President of my own country rode down Laufasvegur in a large black car with the American and Presidential flags flying in the May air.

We welcomed the President to the Residence. He had his picture taken with our family and with the members of the Embassy, all of whom had gathered in front of the adjacent office. He shook hands with every employee, American and Icelandic. As he entered the Residence, Fred, Barbara, and I left for our rooms in the hotel where the White House staff and Cabinet members were staying. Our clothes had gone over earlier in the day. Hotel rooms in Iceland are small; they had kindly given us an extra room just for our clothing.

The summit went well. The visit went well. Nothing marred the display of Iceland's traditional hospitality. Even the Communist ideologue had been persuaded to move his party's anti-American demonstration to a side street where President Nixon did not see it. When Fred thanked him, he answered he didn't do it for Fred or for the United States. "I did it because of Dorothy. She has shown her love for Iceland by learning our language, and even the difficult Rimur poetry we treasure. She and I often discuss this poetry at receptions, you know. I would not do anything to embarrass her."

For three days Iceland had offered only sunny skies. We were glad for the sun, but three days of it meant the Embassy lost its "hardship differential," a pay supplement added because of Iceland's often severe weather conditions. At the airport, still in sunshine we waved goodbye to our visitors. As Air Force One took off to the west, we turned east to drive back to Reykjavík and faced dark clouds. Rain fell before we reached home. It stopped a few hours later when we returned to the NATO Base for our daughter's high school graduation ceremonies. My husband was the graduation speaker, his topic: "A Presidential Visit."

In between the President's departure and Barbara's graduation we moved back into the Residence. Awaiting us was a message in our Guest Book (we had left it open), a thank you note and a gift from President Nixon. Awaiting us, also, were miles of telephone wire (the telephones had been taken). Next to every easy chair we found peppermint lifesavers, Wrigley's gum, a pad and pencil, and a tape recorder; there was a Lawrence Welk record on the player. In the kitchen freezer were seven half gallons of Howard Johnson's coconut ice cream. We shared it with the Embassy staff.

Among the many thank you notes received by the Embassy the following week was one written by the Marine Major on White House stationery. Addressed to me, it read, "You were the best Control Officer we have worked with." I saved it.

Moment of Pride

They played *The Star Spangled Banner* for my husband; for this boy whose Latin translations I had helped with when we were both sophomores in high school; this young flyer I had written to during his months in a POW camp; this man I had married when, together, we had two cars and two hundred dollars (borrowed); this man with whom I had lived in a four story walk-up, a two story walk-up, a single room in a boarding house; this man with whom I had moved from country to country during our Foreign Service career. My husband stepped on to the stage at the Naval Base, and the Navy Band played *The Star Spangled Banner*.

We were in an airplane hangar in Iceland, a hangar emptied of planes to make room for the day's military Change of Command ceremony. A stage erected along one side had a small platform next to it and a ramp connecting the two. Along the hangar's long opposite wall were arranged rows of chairs for the guests. As wife of the U.S. Ambassador, I sat in the front row with the Admiral's wife and members of the Icelandic government.

When the program began, the stage was empty. One at a time, each participating officer stepped onto the platform and stood at attention while a patriotic melody was played. Then the officer turned, faced the stage, and was "piped aboard" by a navy piper. The final officer to enter was the Admiral in Command of the Base. As he stood at attention, the band played a rousing *Anchors Aweigh*, that favorite navy song I had heard on so many occasions thirty years earlier: on the campus of Mount Holyoke College my senior year, as women training to join World War II's Waves marched singing to their classes; from my room on 116th street at New York's Columbia University where I was getting my Master's degree, and new navy officers marched, singing beneath my window; at Military New Year's Eve parties where each of the services would be saluted by its special song. Today the navy salute was played for this tall Admiral in his full dress uniform brightened with gold braid and medals.

Following the Admiral, my husband entered. The only decoration on his dark suit was the caterpillar pin in his lapel, the silkworm symbol of having parachuted out of a plane in an emergency, a decoration earned the day he was shot down over Hungary and became a prisoner-of-war. He stood at attention, the senior U.S. official in Iceland, the personal representative of the President of the United States, and the band played its chosen music of salute. I gasped inside when I heard it. They are playing the National Anthem for Fred. Fortunately the roof of the hangar was high, so my straight spine and glowing head did not bump it. But my heart did. I was sorry our children were not there to share the moment.

During our years of Foreign Service there had been many moments of quiet pride, both at home and abroad. Before leaving for our first post, not knowing what lay ahead, we had agreed that we would return home rather than do anything against our principles. "A career is just a career," we promised each other. Today, as I stood listening to the navy band, I realized my pride had been not just for achievement, but even more for knowing that with this man, integrity and principle came first.

I felt pride when foreign governments recognized this integrity. Iceland's Foreign Minister would say, "Ambassador Irving has been honest in all his dealings with Iceland. I always knew that whatever he said was the truth." Jamaica's Prime Minister put it, "I often disagreed with the American Ambassador, and we enjoyed arguing, but I always knew he was telling me the truth."

I felt pride at home in Washington. When McCarthyism swept the city with its fear of Reds in government, my husband voluntarily testified on behalf of Foreign Service friends wrongly accused of disloyalty. In that era of guilt by association, many felt such support was the first step to dismissal or an ended career. It was easier to be silent. At the Senate hearing of a fellow officer falsely accused of anti-Americanism, we showed our support by sitting in the front row next to the officer's wife.

I was proud when, as director of the program, Fred insisted that the State Department become more aggressive in including traditionally black colleges in their international Cultural Exchange Programs.

Overseas, I felt pride when my husband challenged both the State Department and the Navy to begin sending black members to Iceland. He overruled excuses that black personnel might have trouble finding housing in all-white Iceland, or might upset the sensitive Base negotiations in that country. He went to the Secretary of State and, with Admiral Zumwalt, to the Secretary of Defense to have the policy changed. At the Embassy, the first black family was welcomed into the community and offered a variety of apartments to choose from. On the Base the black servicemen were accepted without a ripple from Iceland.

Indeed my pride in this man had begun on one of our first dates, a day together at a Rhode Island beach. A lost dog near us was suffering from the heat. My husband-to-be would not swim until he had found water and a caretaker for the animal.

When I was a teenager, my mother used to tell me, "Dorothy, when you decide to get married be sure to pick a man you can be proud of. It doesn't matter what work he does, but over the years you will find it will be very important if you can be proud of him."

From that airplane hangar in Iceland, I looked up at the sky and smiled.

Sendiherrafrúin

"Sendiherrarafrúin." The word is not as hard to pronounce as it looks. In Icelandic the emphasis is always on the first syllable of a word. To say *sendiherrafrúin*, you stress the *send-*, then proceed through the next five syllables phonetically: *send-i-herr-a-frú-in*, and you have done it. The universality of the first syllable rule caused me some confusion my first year in Reykjavík. Discussing an upcoming concert, a new friend told me the orchestra would be playing the <u>Mess</u>*-ee-ah*. "Is it played much in the United States?" she asked. Only combined memories of Handel and Christmas enabled my American mind to find its way out of confusion. After a barely noticeable hesitation—during which I moved the emphasis from the *Mess* to the second syllable and changed her *ee* to *i*— could I answer, "Oh, yes, Handel's music is much loved in America, too."

Nor is the word *sendiherrafrúin* difficult to translate. To translate, you start at the end and work backwards. *In* (or *inn* for masculine words) is attached to the end of a noun to mean "the." *Bankinn* is the bank, *bokin*, the book, and *frúin*, the woman or the wife. *Herra* is man and *sendi* denotes the man who is sent, i.e. an ambassador. I was the ambassador's wife.

The first time I heard the term applied to me was on an official visit to the north of Iceland. Our driver was explaining to our local guide, the interests of my husband and myself.

When we passed a school, I heard him say *Sendiherrafrúin*. I liked the sound of it. It has remained my favorite title.

The other word I loved was *sendiherrahjonin*. *Hjonin* means the married couple; the combined word was the ambassadorial married couple. The Icelandic press used it when they wrote about both of us together. A year after we left Iceland, an Icelandic newspaper interviewed us by telephone at our new post in Jamaica. The ensuing article said the reporter had spoken with us both and that *sendiherrahjonin* had sent greetings to all in Iceland

Over the years of a diplomatic life I received a variety of titles. When Fred became the Deputy Ambassador in Vienna, I was addressed as *Frau Minister*. Fred was not a Minister, neither of government nor of anything else, but Austrians thought such a senior position demanded the title. "What are you called in America?" asked a tradesman when I tried to demur. "Mrs. Irving," I answered. "Just Mrs. Irving?" was his unhappy response. I felt (correctly) that I would receive less ostentatious service from him when we met again.

The day we arrived in Iceland, the Embassy's administrative officer asked on behalf of the staff how I wished to be addressed. He did not need to ask about Fred. An ambassador's first name is never used by his staff. Face to face he is always "Mr. Ambassador." When referring to him, he is spoken of as "The Ambassador," or "Ambassador Irving," or sometimes, quietly, as "the boss" or "the old man." Several ambassadors' wives, women whom I respected deeply and who were very effective in their jobs, went by their first names. It just did not seem comfortable to me. "Good evening, Mr. Ambassador, good evening, Dorothy," did not sound like equality. Within the Embassy I became "Mrs. Irving."

The officer who had asked me what I wished to be called, soon approached with another question. At what time of day could he phone me? As the person responsible for the functioning of the Residence, sort of a general manager for the house, he might need to speak with me. Did I have a special time of day I preferred? "Call whenever you wish; if I'm busy or have guests, I'll tell you." When I knew the man better, he said he had asked because at his previous post he had been able to call the wife of the ambassador only between eleven and two. Before eleven she was not up, and after two she had had too much champagne to want to discuss matters concerning the Residence.

The titles became so much a part of us that we have friends from our ambassadorial years who still call us Ambassador and Mrs. Irving, who find it difficult to change to "Fred and Dorothy." This is even true of a couple we write to regularly, and who, themselves, earned the title, *sendiherrahjonin*.

After four years in Reykjavík, we were transferred back to

Washington, only to return to Iceland two months later for our son's wedding there. Rick and Gitte, the daughter of the Danish Ambassador, were married at a small historic church in the countryside outside of Reykjavík. The reception following was held at the Danish Embassy. At the formal dinner, a large U-shaped table seated all the guests: families who had flown in from countries on both sides of the Atlantic, friends in Iceland, the Danish and Icelandic ministers who had conducted the wedding, and the Icelandic couple at whose home Rick and Gitte had met. The bride, the groom, and their parents sat at the head table. The evening became very festive as everyone present made a toast. Rick toasted Gitte in Danish; each of Rick's sisters welcomed Gitte to our family; Fred saluted the new couple. Gitte's father remembered the little girl who had held his hand walking to the bakeshop in Paris each morning. Her sister, her aunt, her university friends, our driver, Rick's college roommate, all rose to toast the pair. I was the last. I, too, stood up to speak. "During my life," I said, "I have had many titles." "One which I treasure deeply was *sendiherrafrúin* which was mine during my very happy four years in this beautiful country. But a title I've had even longer, and which I treasure even more deeply, is one I tonight share with another. If our son will forgive me for omitting him from my toast, I ask you to rise and join me in toasting the new 'Mrs. Irving.'" Barbara said at her end of the table there was not a dry eye.

ALONG THE WAY

In Washington Again

Bara Tia Dropa

"*Bara tia dropa,*" I replied to the waiter offering me more after lunch coffee. The waiter stood silent, silver coffee pot in hand.

"Just a little, please," I revised, remembering where I was—at the British Embassy in Washington D.C. I had recently returned from four years in Iceland, and the Embassy surroundings had transported me back to life in that country where everyone knew what "only ten drops" meant. I still think *tia dropa* when offered more tea or coffee, but I say it only in my own family or with visiting Icelanders.

An Icelandic phrase I use more often is the half question, *Er pad?* "Is that what happened?" "Is that the case?" said with no doubt or criticism implied. It's more a feeling of "I hear what you told me," or "Isn't that interesting?" I like *er pad* for two reasons. It fits so many responses, and when I say it, I picture the Icelandic words. *Er* is spelled *e-r; pad* (pronounced thath*)* is written using two letters we lack in our alphabet. The initial *th* is written like a lower case *p* with its stem extended upwards; the final *th* is like our *d* with a line crossing its upright stem. It makes me happy to picture the words as I say them. When I say *Ekki* (no, or not) I picture the spelling e k k i, but I pronounce it, *e h k k i*, the closest I can come to the ubiquitous Icelandic inhaled *h*. And I remember *Ekki Snertid,* "Do not Touch," from labels on my early visits to the Icelandic National Museum. I remember, but do not use, the helpful Icelandic custom of defining the "we" in a sentence. *Vid, madurinn minn,* "We, my husband and I," made it clear who the "we" was. Other definitions could be "we, my family," "we, my government," "we, my friends." In English, I miss that clarity.

Scraps of language have returned to the States from other posts, too. *Wissen sie?* "Do you know or see?" came home, as did, *Das leben von einem diplomat,* our Viennese driver's sympathetic words when we complained about Vienna's intense social life. The words are called on now when we know we must take part in something we'd rather skip. To say, *Das Leben von* means duty is calling. In Vienna, *Gnadige Frau*, "noble woman," was used for women of high birth or whose husbands held a high position. A storekeeper, all but bowing, would ask me, "Would the *gnadige Frau* like to see anything else?" In our family the term means a woman with an exaggerated sense of her own importance. Sometimes it refers to a granddaughter becoming very fancy. "She's going to be a *gnadige Frau*, that one." For a long time the most useful Viennese phrase was *nicht wahr*? "Is it not so?" or, "aren't you?" *Nicht wahr* need not agree in number with the item to which it refers. "The train will be late; you have the tickets; they are going downtown." *Nicht wahr* can follow them all. Our use of it has faded over time. *Gerade Aus* remains with us. *Gerade aus*, "straight ahead," in traffic or in life; the way to get to where you are going.

At Burger King today, the coffee cup warned, "Hot be careful," in four languages (no Icelandic or Jamaican patois here). The German caught my eye. "*Vorsicht, heiss.*" *Vorsicht* has become so much a family word, I had forgotten it was foreign. *Vorsicht*, there's a hole in the road; *vorsicht*, the ice is slippery, the stove is hot.

From New Zealand we brought home only one word, "beauty," used as an adjective. It rings with special truth to say, "that's a beauty dress." Perhaps the jarring of the word's misuse makes us notice it more, makes the admiration seem more genuine. We did not bring home the New Zealand definition of homely to mean homelike, nor their abhorrence of bloody as a vulgar swear word.

From Jamaica, our life is enriched by proverbs. "New broom sweep clean but old broom knows the corners." From Jamaica we treasure their lovely farewell, "Walk good."

My mind carries something of German, Icelandic, and Jamaican patois. Recently, I learned how my brain ranks the three. I had studied German in school and spoken it during two tours in Vienna. Later I lived in Jamaica and in Iceland. At Kennedy airport on our interterminal bus, a German traveler was seeking help. I told him I spoke some German, and realized only during my offered directions that I was speaking half in German and half in Icelandic. I hope the man got where he was trying to go. As soon as I turned off English, Icelandic had rushed to the fore. The experience confirmed what I had often heard: your most recent or strongest foreign language will squeeze any others into third place or fourth.

I do not know how people who are multilingual manage, how they select from their many ways of saying, "Please. Thank you. Can you help me?" Do they have phrases of each language that enrich their daily lives? that bring an inner smile at the memory of where the words were learned? that bond them to a distant world? Do any words make their statement more exact? If they use *bara tia dropa* in the wrong place, are they embarrassed or are they smiling inside?

I Won't Go In

Because I loved it, I don't want to go back. Not inside. Not to see the rooms I once knew so well. Is the furniture rearranged, recovered; are the walls painted, the drapes changed? I don't want to know. I don't mind that someone else lives there now; it's right that they do, but I don't want to see what they've done. I don't want to go inside.

In our four years in Iceland, the Ambassador's residence became my home, my most loved home. Not as royal as the actual palace we inhabited in Vienna; in that city and that ornate home, I felt like an actress in an operetta. In New Zealand, our government house had been flat and plain; it was never part of us. The Jamaican plantation type house with its large grounds and staff of six was a lovely Ambassador's residence, but we felt like temporary tenants. Even our earlier suburban Washington homes hold bonds only because of family memories, not because of the houses. But from the first day, the white cement house on Reykjavík's Laufasvegur welcomed us. From the first day I felt at home.

The living room furniture covered in gold and white was welcoming and bright in that land of long winters. Above the white couch the large gold-framed mirror gave added light. Along a side wall a pair of white-covered revolving chairs turned next to a round table. Above them hung two of the Arts in Embassy paintings we had chosen. Of course, those paintings are gone; they have to be. American artists lend their works for temporary display in the public rooms of the residence. Pieces are selected by each new ambassador, and stay only for that ambassador's term. The pieces my husband and I had chosen before leaving Washington had hung so comfortably in this house: a large painting, "The Girl With a Boat" at the foot of the stairs, a Frank Stella square in the dining room hall, the Brockie Stevenson line drawings of New England on the side living room wall. When we left Iceland, we purchased the two Stevenson drawings. They now hang in our New England living room. Four Theo Naos pressed pieces lined the stairs making that entry a small gallery. Over the piano, Helen Frankenthaler's painting of pansy leaves brought green to match the soft green of two side chairs at the far end of the room. Into that lovely room came much of Iceland, and in time I felt as if the room became me and I became the room.

Has a new family changed the chintz on the small sofa in the second living room, the room with the dramatic Icelandic designed fireplace in its center? A knee-high hearth held the fire, visible from two sides. Above it rose the gray cement chimney, dense with rocks near its base, rocks that spread ever more sparsely as the chimney climbed upward. After seeing my first volcano spewing rocks into the air, I appreciated anew the beauty of this fireplace. That it had no place for Christmas stockings seemed a small price to pay for such originality and beauty. We laid our stockings on both sides along its hearth.

This room was where our children gathered when they came home; where our son persuaded the daughter of the Danish Ambassador to marry him and move to the States; where President Nixon sat with his sore legs up on the chintz covered hassock, especially made for his visit. It was also the room that held my special haven: a golden wing chair tucked into a corner next to a bookcase, a lamp table by its side. When I had fifteen minutes, or maybe thirty, free, I sat in that corner almost out of sight. I read the Icelandic history books shelved there or one of my own favorites brought from home. Deep in a book, I briefly escaped the day's responsibilities and then returned refreshed.

In the first floor guest cloakroom we hung wood framed tiles of New England's Sturbridge Village. Each Christmas in the adjacent entry hall two golden reindeer from Thailand stood on the half moon table. Made by Thai craftsmen who had never seen a reindeer, sent by a friend stationed at the American Embassy in Bangkok, they welcomed the holiday to our northern home. In the upper hall on the marble topped table two single roses stood in crystal bud vases at the side of the guest book. Between parties the guest book was closed, and the hall flowers might be a plant.

One item, which has probably remained, is the long dining room table, made for that room before our time. It stretched the length of the room, a beautiful sight when silver, crystal, and bowls of flowers glowed along the damask cloth. Because we found the table's length overwhelming for daily use, we had lifted out the center leaves and moved them with their own stand to the far end of the room. With a bowl of flowers, it filled the room nicely and left the shorter table less overwhelming for small dinners or luncheons for two.

I won't worry about what happened to the bedrooms, but are there still two desks in the upstairs study? My husband's faced the wall; mine, by the window overlooked a Reykjavík street. The phone was on my desk. I felt as if its wires reached all over Reykjavík, into homes of all political parties, into the Icelandic Red Cross, the Icelandic Federation of University Women, to the homes of cabinet ministers, to teachers, to librarians, to the new friends I had made. Each Monday morning I used it to plan my week. Does the room still have a lounge chair and stool for a last-at-home child, a teenage daughter who uses the foot-stooled chair in the corner while her parents work at their desks?

If I'm in Reykjavík, I'll be invited into the house. For the sake of courtesy and protocol I will have to go in, though I would rather not. But I have a plan. If I look just at the people and not the rooms, perhaps nothing will blur my memories. If I do not let the new living room superimpose itself on my mind, I can continue to carry the picture of that house I so loved. Or perhaps I'll just leave my memories outside the door and pick them up as I leave.

There Are No Ants In Iceland

(While reviewing a book for use by middle school children I came upon this phrase. My poem is the result.)

There are no ants in Iceland.
I just learned that today.
As long as I've known and loved that land,
I never knew this before.
There are no ants in Iceland.

It's true, I never saw an ant when camping out on lava,
Or picnicking on deep soft moss, or drinking from a stream.
It's true, I never saw an ant in kitchen or in pantry,
On window or on sidewalk, or climbing on the grass.
But, still I never realized:
There are no ants in Iceland.

There are no ants in Iceland.
Who does what ants should do?
Without them, what is left undone?
I think we need to know.
Perhaps a study's needed here.
Maybe I should make it.
If science calls, then I must go
Back to that land I loved.
To see: Why not?
    What if?
    and Why?
    There are no ants in Iceland.

D. C. Day Care

I was not accepted the first three months I worked at the Day Care Center. I was greeted politely, given instructions, but not looked on as part of the team. When my co-workers went out for coffee after work, I was not invited.

I could not blame them. Here I was, a white woman from suburban Washington, working three days a week for free at a job these women of color did five days a week for a necessary salary. I viewed Social Work as a way of reaching out. They viewed it as a way of getting out—out of the poverty into which they had been born, of the neglected part of the city in which they lived. Of course, they didn't accept me.

Our family was in Washington between Foreign Service assignments. Fred had been appointed by the President to be Assistant Secretary of State for Oceans, International Environmental and Scientific Affairs. He went immediately to his office in the State Department. I looked around for what I would do. Since we never knew how long we'd be home, taking a full time job seemed unfair to an employer and to other job seekers. At the D.C. Volunteer Center I asked for suggestions. I had taught and done considerable work with children, I said. My one request was to work in a racially integrated group, and, I hoped, under the direction of an adult of color. In Washington in the 1970s, children had little opportunity to see black people supervising white people. One way I could use my months at home was to give children this experience.

The interviewer at the Volunteer Center described an opening. "There is a new experimental testing program for nursery school children in day care centers. The three social workers doing it could use a fourth person part time. The job matches your requirements. Are you interested? I should tell you that this is a section of D.C. with a very high crime rate." My older daughter, when I told her where I was working, would say, "You're working WHERE?" I assured her I would be fine, and I was.

In October, I became a social worker with the Early Periodic Screening and Diagnostic Testing Program (EPSDT) of the D.C. Nursery schools. The work consisted of picking up a testing kit at the EPSDT Center, driving to the assigned school, and one by one taking each child to a separate room to play specified games which measured abilities and understanding. With my nursery school experience, I was able to put most of the children at ease. At the end of each day, the four social workers took our notes back to headquarters and wrote our reports.

The others could see I was dependable, almost always cheerful, and after some weeks they got used to me. But still, I was never asked to join them for coffee.

Finally, in the fourth month there was a breakthrough. It happened in two stages. First, was the matter of the testing sets. Of the four sets, one was superior, two middling, and one mismatched and less inviting, distinctions I had not noticed. On my early arrival one morning, I picked up the first set I saw and left for my school. I returned that afternoon to face a very angry co-worker. "How could you take the newest set? You know, that's the one I always use. How could you do that?" My regret at upsetting her was so genuine that I gained enough good will to be almost accepted. There was still no coffee, but daily greetings became warmer.

The following week I lost my purse. I had gone to my car after work, my car keys in my hand at the ready. In this area of Washington, I was never frightened in the morning, but in the late afternoon we were all told to take precautions. Unemployed people may have spent the day drinking, would not be hospitable, and could be unpleasant. On this day, I unlocked my car, stepped in, locked the door and then realized I did not have my purse. Where could it be? The only place I could think of was in front of the Center. The Director constantly emphasized that we must lock the door carefully behind us each time we left the Center. This day in order to use both hands on the lock, I had put my purse on the ground. I did not remember picking it up. Was it still sitting there, just to the left of the main front door? I groaned.

Quickly re-locking the car, I hurried back to see nothing on the grass by the door. I had not really expected the purse to be there. I went upstairs to see if I had left it in our room. It was not there. I was about to leave, discouraged, telling myself to be more careful next time.

"Dorothy," came a voice from across the hall, "Did you lose your purse?"

"Yes, I must have left it sitting outside."

"Well, I found one and brought it in. I put it behind that screen. See if it's yours."

It was. As soon as I identified it, I gave the finder a big hug of joy. I was so relieved. She was equally pleased for me.

The next afternoon I was invited for coffee. Had it been the hug, the foolishness in leaving my purse on the ground, the willingness to apologize for taking the "good" set of testing material? I never asked. I had delicious coffee, long conversations, and new friendships grew.

Late in the spring, my supervisor, a young woman about thirty five, came to me and said she had obtained funding and could now hire another full time paid social worker. Would I work full time? I thanked her most sincerely, but told her that because of family responsibilities I really could do only three days a week. The next day she returned and said her boss had agreed to split the job in half if I would take the three-day part. I was deeply touched.

However it was not to be. Two weeks later my husband received assignment as Ambassador to Jamaica, beginning in June. The EPSDT team of social workers all came to the swearing in ceremony, a formal event held in the diplomatic reception rooms on the seventh floor of the Department of State. They watched me hold the Bible as my husband took his oath of office. It made my day complete to see them there. They had been an important part of my year's stay in Washington.

JAMAICA 1977-79

Our last Post

Assignment: Jamaica

We almost didn't go to Jamaica. After twenty-five years in the Foreign Service, with its packing, unpacking, moving, we were considering staying in our own country. The four years in Iceland had been so satisfactory to us both, we knew it would be hard to surpass that experience. In the year since our return home, Fred had had offers from two universities and had interviewed for the presidency of the United Nations Association.

He had also been approached about another ambassadorship, but we were not tempted. The thought of living in our own country had great appeal. A Saturday morning phone call changed our minds. Fred took the call in our bedroom where I was ironing and he was sorting papers. I heard him answer, "Yes. Yes, I see." Then a long silence on his side followed by, "Let me talk it over with Dorothy. I'll call you back tomorrow."

"That was State Department, the Undersecretary. They really want us to go to Jamaica. He said Jamaican-U.S. relations have become so strained, there could easily be a break between the two countries. State Department is afraid that if we break with Jamaica, we'll have a second Cuba right on our southern doorstep. He also said our Embassy in Jamaica is one of the worst run anywhere. We could just go for a year or two. If we can't turn it around in that time, it will be hopeless, anyway."

Fred paused. We knew that the man who had been the Embassy's Administrative Officer in Iceland was now in Jamaica. Together we phoned his Kingston home. The officer confirmed the place was a mess and that relations with the United States were at a very low ebb. "We could certainly use you both," he said, "and I personally would be delighted."

This Too Is Diplomacy

We discussed it that afternoon and evening, but in our hearts we knew our decision. Sunday morning Fred called the Undersecretary and said we'd be willing to go, but would want to plan on no more than the two years he had mentioned. "Great," was the reply. "We're relieved. Jamaica's Prime Minister, Michael Manley, has insisted he wants a career Foreign Service Officer this time. We'll be counting on you to make a difference."

The White House was glad to have it settled and, once they had our "yes," sent the name to Jamaica for that country's agrément. Usually sending an agrément is just a formality. Most countries do not wish to offend the sending country by declining an offered ambassador; consent to the nomination often comes back within hours or a day. This was not the case with Jamaica, and who could blame them? The previous two ambassadors had been political appointees, given their posts as rewards for large political contributions to President Nixon's campaign.

The first of these was heard to complain that he was angry to have been given Jamaica; he thought he had given enough money to merit Austria. When Michael Manley took office, this Ambassador went to pay the expected courtesy call on the new Prime Minister. When Manley held out his hand to greet him, our man declined the PM'S hand saying, "It's not personal, Mr. Prime Minister, but I don't shake hands with black people." My husband and I wondered with whom he had socialized. We learned it was the few white wealthy citizens of the country, the all-white Jamaican Yacht Club, and the European members of the diplomatic corps. This Ambassador owned a huge yacht to which he had affixed the seal of the United States. I was deeply offended to hear this. The seal of the United States is for official use only. It is not a personal possession.

During the second year of his tour, this Ambassador was called to Washington for a conference on drug problems in the Caribbean. Testifying at a Senate hearing, he was asked if he foresaw any problem with Jamaica over drug laws. At that open hearing, with press and cameras present, the American Ambassador told the Senators not to worry. "There will be no problem with Jamaica," he assured them. "I have Michael Manley in my pocket." Regardless of the fact that Michael Manley was a man no one ever had "in his pocket," to make such a statement in a public hearing was both rude and stupid.

Of course, word reached Jamaica. Immediately after his return, the Ambassador was PNG'ed, declared "persona non grata" and asked to leave the country. Sending home the representative from another government is an act not taken lightly. After my husband and I had been in Jamaica several months, a member of the Jamaican Foreign Office identified himself to us as the one who had delivered the PNG notification to the Office of the Ambassador. He found it hard to hide his pride at the role he played.

The replacement American Ambassador was also a man of wealth. He, too, was given the Ambassadorship as a reward for a large political contribution. He spent much of his time playing polo, and, like his predecessor, resented Jamaica all during his stay. His wife regularly told other Embassy wives that she realized Kingston was terrible; they should just get away to the beaches in the north. This couple, too, mixed only with the white members of Jamaican society, with Yacht Club members, and with appropriate diplomats. During Manley's campaign for reelection, the Ambassador openly campaigned for Manley's opponent and encouraged other Embassy members to do the same. Foreign Service Officers are not allowed to interfere in the internal affairs of a country. They may have hopes about who wins an election, but they absolutely may not try to influence the decision. Fortunately this man's tour ended soon with the change of administration and a new president in Washington.

With this history, it was not surprising that Manley's government took some time to return their country's agrément. Fred and I were not offended that they had us both investigated as to our racial attitudes, or that the investigation was helped by friends of Jamaica at Howard University, Washington's historically black college. Nor were we worried as to the answers they would receive.

After a week Jamaica's consent came back. The last hurdle was Fred's hearing before the Senate Foreign Relations Committee. This went smoothly, and we began to shop, plan, and pack. The State Department offered us a clothing allowance to help with the shift from northern Iceland to tropical Jamaica: $175 a person! Once again we separated our possessions into storage and take-with piles. We sent the grandfather's clock and the piano to our older daughter. The canoe went to our son's house. In July we left for Jamaica, wondering what welcome we would meet in that tense and troubled land.

Reports on our activities had preceded us, and our welcomes were widespread and cautiously warm. Later, Jamaican friends would tell us that during our first months in their country we had been watched carefully for signs of racial prejudice.

Shortly after our arrival, my husband and I were invited to a reception at the Jamaican Yacht Club. We lost some face there when the white-trousered, blue-blazered members learned that we had no yacht. But they were not so nonplussed as to prevent their nodding to us that they were sure we would continue our two predecessors' practice of ensuring that all their friends could get visas to the United States whenever they wished. Fred told them an Ambassador could not control visas. It was our only visit to the Club.

The famous yacht had already been mentioned. At their first meeting, the Prime Minister asked the new American Ambassador, "Tell me, Mr. Ambassador, do you own a yacht?" "No, Mr. Prime Minister," my husband answered, "just a canoe." Then he added truthfully, "Not that I wouldn't like to have a yacht." Both men smiled. It was the beginning of a mutually respectful liking for each other.

Many months later an American monthly speaking of improvement in U.S.-Jamaican relations, wrote, "Americans are no longer stoned on the streets, but welcomed as friends. The most influential foreigner in Kingston is the U.S. Ambassador, Frederick Irving, who neither plays polo nor treats the Jamaicans with disrespect." [1]

And, Mrs. Irving's Jamaican doctor (also doctor to the Prime Minister) would say to a group in Kingston, "The thing about Mrs. Irving is that she thinks everyone is alike."

---

[1] From an article "Killing Jamaica With Kindness," by T.D. Ailman. Copyright © 1979 by Harper's Magazine. All rights reserved. Reproduced from the May issue by special permission.

Security In A Tense Land

1977 in Jamaica was a time of shortages: shortage of food, of jobs, of money; shortage of hope. No shortage of frustration, of uneasiness, of resentment; no shortage of violence. Fear and tension were prevalent.

Our introduction to this came our first night. My husband and I were staying at the home of the Deputy Chief of Mission. He pointed to the barred windows in the bath and our bedroom and showed us where he hung the key to the full sized grilled door which "protected" this area. The door, which he called a "rape door," prevented entry to the bedroom wing from the rest of the house. "We lock this when we go to bed," he said. "You can't be too careful in Jamaica just now." We both felt he was overreacting. We did not plan to be afraid.

The following week we received a second warning. After meeting for lunch downtown, my husband and I walked back the three blocks to the tall office building where our Embassy occupied two floors. As we left the elevator and entered Fred's office, the local police chief was already on the phone. "Please don't do that again, sir. It isn't safe for you and Mrs. Irving to walk through the city. Please use your official car next time."

The official car was big, black, heavy, and safe. The security it offered was a mixed blessing. The car's windows, made of bulletproof glass, could not be opened. This was hardly friendly. If Jamaicans were seeing us off after a visit, we could not wind down the windows to wave or say goodbye. Also, in Jamaica's tropical climate, a car that had stood idle for a few hours became stifling. When we asked to have the windows replaced, the Department of State said we had to keep them unless Fred would take full responsibility for giving them up. His request would have to be in writing, and his letter would be kept on file in Washington. (Was this in case we were shot? I wondered.) Fred's letter to the Secretary of State read: "I hereby voluntarily decline the use of bullet proof windows in my official car. Respectfully, sir, I think my chances of death by suffocation are much greater than my chances of getting shot." The windows were replaced, and both handclasps and air could pass through the newly opened space.

The greatest protection was our driver, Mr. Hudson, who had been trained in security matters in the army. It was he who drove my husband or me into downtown neighborhoods, where political gang warfare was intense and often violent. Housing projects in the city were controlled by the two major political parties, and open fighting took place between their rival gangs. When I was going to schools in such neighborhoods or in remote sections of the country, the Embassy was reassured if Mr. Hudson was driving. A week after I visited one inner city school, a battle ending in two deaths erupted three blocks from where Mr. Hudson had parked our car. "Lucky thing we went last week," was his only comment. Murders occurred in all parts of the city. One week there was a body in front of the Embassy building every day. A brand new Foreign Service wife, three days in a row, passed a corpse while driving her husband to work. Badly shaken, she asked to return to the States. My husband let them transfer.

We had security at our home, too, but there, again, it was a mixed blessing. The Ambassador's Residence stood on six acres of ground with a swimming pool, a large garden, a guest house, staff quarters, and the main house, all surrounded by an easily climbable fence. Like most homes ours had grillwork on all the windows. At least ours were decorative; the iron was curved into a design of leaves and flowers.

For twenty-four hours a day, two guards holding rifles stood at the gate of the property to screen anyone entering the driveway. Should anything untoward happen in the house, we had only to bump the receiver off a red emergency phone and a guard would come immediately. One night while turning down our bed, I noticed the red phone off its base. I must have done it when lifting clothes out of the closet.

Immediately I rang the gate. "There is no emergency; I bumped the phone by mistake. I'm sorry."

"That's all right, ma'am," he answered politely. "It's been off for a few hours, but we were sure it was an accident."

The same guards were more attentive when our children on holiday from college would swim in the Residence pool. One guard, after making his hourly rounds of the grounds would stand about twenty feet from the pool, loaded rifle in hand.

"You may go back to the gate, now." I said when I saw him.

"I want to be sure they're safe," he answered, unmoving. I stood my five feet two motherliness next to his six feet one uniformed guardedness (the red police stripe down his black pants made him seem even taller). I spoke firmly, "You must return to the gate now. They are safe." We stood thus briefly. I had not been a teacher and a mother of three for nothing. The guard returned to the gate.

Until the day I visited a camp for inner city children about two hours into the countryside, I had not realized the Jamaican Government was trying to protect me everywhere. This protection was never at my request; I would have preferred not to have it. At the close of my day at the camp, one teacher said. "I've never seen police cars out here in the country before. Today I've seen four. What do you think has happened?" "It's Mrs. Irving's visit," the experienced director answered, and it was. The head of Government Security later complained to Fred that my trips and school visits "all over the island" were taking up too much of his staff's time. "Does she have to do so much?" "She has to." Fred replied.

Despite the frequent shootings and the constant presence of guards to remind me, only twice did I feel nervous or very uneasy. Once was at a reception given by a Jamaican family whose home was in the hills above Kingston. The hosts, good people, devoted to their country, had a gathering of government, business, and diplomatic guests. As at most Jamaican parties this one flowed out of the house into the garden. As I stood there talking to another guest we both heard the whirr of a low flying helicopter above us. Its searchlight illuminated our group. "I guess they haven't caught him yet," my companion said, "I heard he was headed towards the hills." A prisoner had escaped from detention and was apparently chased to this area. I was not afraid for myself, but the thought of the man being pursued by police planes while we partied below made me shudder.

The time I was nervous for myself occurred in a Jamaican home.

One member of the Jamaican cabinet was so anti-American he would not even speak to anyone from the American Embassy. The Embassy was eager to establish contact with him in the hopes of modifying his views. At a large dinner one evening the cabinet officer's wife was seated next to Fred. Knowing she was a teacher, Fred mentioned that I had been a teacher at home and he was sure I would enjoy talking with her. A few weeks later, she phoned to invite me to lunch. She would send her car for me, she offered. At the appointed time a small black sedan pulled up to the house, and a young man came in to escort me. Our butler, opening the door, looked very dubious at this escort. The young man led me to the car, and we sat together in the back. A revolver lay on the seat next to him. In the front next to the driver sat another young man, a revolver lying openly in his lap. As we rode down the long driveway that wound through our yard, I seriously considered these revolvers and wondered if I could suddenly feign illness and cancel this trip.

When we reached the teacher's home, my escort led me into the living room. The other two men followed us and joined three young men standing around the walls of the room. All wore T-shirts, work pants, and the wool knit hats of the "revolutionaries," and all were visibly armed. Except for asking one of them to bring us each an iced tea, my hostess ignored them. I took my cue from her. She and I sat on the couch and talked for about forty minutes. Then she said she wanted to take me to a very remote restaurant she liked, "one not many people know about. My car will take us." The remoteness of the unknown restaurant plus the presence of the revolvers, made me once again consider sudden illness, but knowing how important this contact could be for the Embassy, I smiled and entered the car.

The country restaurant was not far from her home. Frankly, I don't remember the food. What I do remember was our three and a half hour conversation there. She had many questions and supposed grievances about the CIA and about America's plans in the region. Some of her thoughts were so extreme it was not hard to disprove them. "That would just not make sense," I convinced her on more than one count. Other cases held a kernel of truth, and I tried to make clear the ideals and intent of my own country. I sent a silent thank you back to the State Department for granting me a full security clearance, so I had facts to back up my answers. I worked very hard for the three and a half hours but when we returned to her house, she hugged me warmly. "Thank you," she said, "I feel for the first time that I know your country now." Our relations were cordial from then on, and I never again met the circle of young guards when I visited her. The Embassy was delighted at the breakthrough.

That day was the closest I came to being afraid. Fred and I both knew that an act of violence was possible and could occur at any time. It would not happen at his office, because the Embassy Marines confiscated all knives and guns before anyone went in to see the Ambassador. Some days they gathered quite a number. It would not happen in our gated, grilled, and guarded home. From the beginning we had to choose between living in these protected environments or in the community. We were glad we chose the community.

Bonnie

I hold in my hand the small index card given to me by the Ambassador's secretary the day we arrived in Jamaica. Typed on it in three columns are six names, six salaries, six job titles: "Names of Household Help at the American Ambassador's Residence." I scanned the list, bottom to top: gardener, laundress, waiter, cleaning woman, cook, butler. I groaned at the word, "Butler."

Once before we had briefly had a butler—in Iceland, that most democratic of countries. Geoffrey and his wife, Muriel, had come from England as a cook-butler team. They must have come from an old-fashioned British home with many servants and a system of rank both above and below stairs. They could never adjust to our lack of a large household staff, or to the informality of our family. Perhaps when they agreed to come to us, they thought the title, "Ambassador," would make us prestigious enough to be worthy of them.

When we asked Geoffrey how he wished us to address him, he said he was sometimes called Geoffrey or more often by his last name: Smith, no mister in front of it. It was sort of a Jeeves approach. But this was no Jeeves. Jeeves had put his employer first. Geoffrey put Geoffrey first. Geoffrey wore different uniforms for each household task: black jacket for polishing, blue for dusting, lighter blue for answering the door, white for serving. His methods of work were as rigid as his choice of uniform. If I absentmindedly rearranged objects he had dusted on the living room coffee table, he was so upset that he had to mention it and rearrange the appearance. Muriel had only two uniforms: white for cooking, blue for cleaning up. Unfortunately she could not cook. Our coexistence did not last long.

I tried to be open minded about another butler. This man had been with the home three years.

Each Embassy is allotted a staff appropriate to the size of the residence, the climate, (it is harder to work fast in the tropics), the extent of the garden, etc. Often, such household help stay indefinitely from one American family to the next. Of the six in Jamaica, the Ambassador's secretary told us, "The two senior men, Bonnie and Bob, live in staff quarters on the grounds. The others come five days a week. They will come more often if you have house guests."

"Bonnie will be waiting at the door," said the young Embassy officer who escorted us on our first visit to our new home. When our car drove up the long driveway, Bonnie opened the front door. Dressed in black pants, short sleeve white shirt, black bow tie, he looked too young for his official title, "Butler," but even on that first meeting he exhibited the self respect and professionalism he had earned as a graduate of Jamaica's esteemed hotel school. I trusted him immediately, and I trusted him ever after.

Bonnie always stood at the door when we left on a trip and would be standing there again when we returned. I soon knew that as long as he was there, the home would be cared for, protected, respected. Unlike Geoffrey, he was willing to do anything for us, and was able to do it all in a white shirt and black pants. When we lacked a cook, Bonnie and the woman who cleaned, together, made the meals. We still make "Bonnie's Pumpkin Soup," and broil, "Bonnie's Chicken," but we have never been able to approach his iced tea, my life-saving drink those hot Jamaican days. He always had some ready when I came in from a day visiting schools.

When I had the mother of the gardener to coffee, Bonnie served us as professionally and as graciously as he had the Prime Minister's mother the day before. When the two very young teachers from the Rastafarian school came to tea, he ignored their excited "Oohs" as they looked around our beautiful living room. Bonnie's home was in a town west of Kingston, where his wife was a teacher. Later hers would be one of the many Jamaican schools I would visit for a day. That summer of our arrival they were expecting their first child.

On this first day, I asked him to show me around and tell me what everyone did.

"We would like you to continue as you have until we see how it works. My husband and I will be in Washington for about two weeks before we return. Can you think of anything needed at the Residence that I might buy during that time?" I knew the previous two ambassadors had been political appointees. These are often people of wealth who bring many of their own things with them, and when they leave such items go with them. From earlier experience, I had learned it was best to check on what gaps might exist. Together, Bonnie and I looked at equipment and went over kitchen and household supplies. Then I asked to see the quarters where he and Bob lived and where the others gathered for rest periods during their day. "Please tell the others and let me know when they are ready."

Ten minutes later Bonnie returned to the den. "If you would like to come now?" He led me fifty feet across the yard to the one-story building known as staff quarters. It held two small bedrooms, a bath, a larger room full of crates and boxes.

We went into Bonnie's bedroom first.

"Do you need anything here?"

"I could use another sheet."

"How many do you have now?"

He immediately backtracked, "Oh, I do have two. It's only a problem if it rains on the day we do laundry. I really don't need more."

I swallowed hard. Two sheets for a bed, when in the linen closet I had just counted six opened sets of sheets and twelve unopened pairs for two guest rooms. Sears brand, white, no-iron.

"You should have more than two. How about a spread? If I see a spread, what color would you like?"

"I like blue," he answered, with the first hint of a smile.

The room next to Bonnie's belonged to the gardener/waiter, Bob, who preferred green for his spread. I asked about the larger room across the hall, now full of boxes and crates.

"The boxes are empty. They were left by the last Ambassador. We were told to save them in case you would want them." It was clear that the room was meant to be a staff living room.

"Where does the staff eat meals?" I asked. In large homes in Jamaica it was customary to have a separate staff dining room, or a large table in the kitchen. This kitchen was so small it would barely hold two people standing up. It would not hold a table.

"We used to have a staff dining room," he showed me the space, "but the last Ambassador needed that room for storage, so now we eat here." "Here" was a fold up wooden shelf attached to the outside of the kitchen wall. It was in a narrow passageway connecting front and back yards. When the three stools pushed against the wall were pulled out for eating, anyone going from front to back yards had to squeeze around the eaters.

Before leaving the house that day I sent over two new sets of sheets for each bed. I arranged to have the boxes and crates removed from the sitting room. When we returned from Washington, I brought bedspreads in blue and green, matching cotton rugs for bedside use, and new pillows for the beds. It took little to restore the now empty sitting room to an inviting rest spot for a hard working staff: a TV from embassy storage, an extra chair, a couch not being used, a simple rug. A kitchen table and chairs and a refrigerator made the staff dining room a happy mealtime gathering place. A stove was already there.

We had the staff shower repaired, the toilet fixed. There was a separate toilet room for the Jamaican security guards at the gate. I would be ill to describe what it looked like when we first saw it. We installed a soap dish, a sink, a rack for paper towels, and a paper holder for toilet paper. The pile of torn newspapers on the floor was thrown out.

I thought a lot about the condition of staff quarters. What did it say about the Americans who lived in the big house? The best I can believe is that they never stepped into the rooms where their household staff lived and didn't know; but shouldn't they have known? These Jamaicans worked every day in the Ambassador's home, they took care of the lovely furnishings there, they served the guests who came. They lived right there on Embassy property. Did the resident American family feel no concern about how they lived?

I thought about this when the wife of a departing Embassy member came to pay a farewell call. In the 1970s such calls were no longer necessary, but I was always glad to see anyone who wished to come. "I'm sorry we won't overlap longer," she said. "I can see you are someone who will get involved in Jamaica. I'm sorry I didn't do more."

I knew this woman had had a very difficult past two years. A parent had died. One son had been very ill; the other had been in serious trouble, not of his making. I imagined she had needed all her energy just to keep going.

"You did what you had to do first." I answered. "Do not feel badly. There are years when we have to be centered in our homes." Then she told me about an embroidered tablecloth one of her helpers had made for her as a farewell gift: full sized with twelve napkins. "It's really beautiful." Suddenly I saw the kind of person she was.

"Do not think that you did nothing here to reach out. Imagine how many hours your helper spent making that cloth for you in her home or her yard; how she spoke of her American employer as she worked, how many of her neighbors came to know of your kindness, and that your Jamaican helper cared enough about you to spend her free time in this way. Do not think you did nothing for your country." "The Ambassador can make a speech, and everyone thinks it's because he's the Ambassador, but word of how we treat our helpers spreads through the community, and paints its own picture of America."

And the image of how our helpers treat us spreads through our hearts and colors our picture of Jamaica.

After we'd been in Jamaica about a year, that country's largest newspaper, The *Jamaican Sunday Gleaner*, ran a two-page article about my activities in schools and social service agencies. I cut out a copy, and wrote a note: "To Bonnie, Sylvia, Bob, Vincent, Leona—Thank you all. I could not have done all this without your help." It was true. If I had done all the cooking, the cleaning and laundering, the changing of beds for guests, the serving of meals, of cold drinks, teas and coffees; not to mention the gardening needed to keep our grounds beautiful, I could not, also, have visited schools all over Jamaica. I could not have consulted with teachers and social workers and members of the government.

I smiled as I scotch taped the clipping and my message on the wall of the staff dining room.

Our departing gift to Bonnie was to have him put on the regular Embassy payroll, thus earning him benefits and job insurance. The day we left I told him I knew we were leaving the house in good hands. Bonnie did not come to the airport to see us off. "I must finish my work here," he said, busy in the pantry. We both had tears in our eyes.

A Cup Of Tea

It was not easy to have an evening cup of tea in Jamaica. We dismissed the household staff after dinner, and usually my husband and I wanted nothing more. But some evenings, after working an hour or two at our desks, we felt a cup of tea would be nice. It hardly seemed kind or necessary to ask a staff member to return. I was a grown woman; I had kept house in the States. I could certainly produce a cup of tea on my own. But producing it here was a challenge.

From our study, I walked down the home's lovely curved staircase into the front hall, walked the length of the formal dining room, and entered the pantry. The pantry held two refrigerators, a serving table, shelves of canned goods, but no stove. Next I passed the long narrow room where dishes got washed in two side-by-side sinks, and came to the back door.

At night every outside door of the house was locked. Taking the keys from inside a cupboard, I opened the back door and stepped down one step onto the outside path that separated the kitchen building from the main house. I unlocked the kitchen door, banged on it several times, then reached my hand in quickly and flipped on the light switch. Immediately closing the door, I waited fifteen seconds. Noise, light, and fifteen seconds gave the cockroaches time to escape to wherever cockroaches hide. After the fifteen seconds, I could enter the kitchen, see nary an insect, and believe (almost) none had ever been there.

Still in pursuit of the tea, I rinsed out a pan and put water on to boil. While it heated, I unscrewed the glass jar holding tea bags, removed two, and rescrewed the cover tightly. I rinsed out two cups, put it all on a tray, poured in the boiling water, and retraced my steps across the outdoor path to the back door. I put the tray on the pantry table and returned to lock both opened doors.

At the kitchen door, I sent a message to the roaches, "It's all yours until morning. Have a nice night." I returned the keys to the cupboard, picked up the tray and, turning off lights as I went, mounted the beautiful staircase to our sitting room and study.

As we sipped our tea, I found myself remembering our first fourth floor walk-up in Washington, D.C. There the kitchen had been a converted closet right off the one room we had rented. Smaller than an Ambassador's Residence, but rather more convenient.

The Button Basket

On her tenth birthday I gave Emilie the Button Basket. Not the buttons it once held—those I poured into a yellow plastic bowl, which took the basket's place on my bedroom table. Folded in the bottom of the basket I left the green florist's paper that had come with it.

The basket is pretty, made of thin strips of polished aluminum woven to look like a small version of a straw garden basket, the kind used to gather flowers or vegetables. The aluminum handle curves from one side to the other and can be folded down if desired.

For many years, before Emilie was born, the basket was used to hold the extra buttons a home accumulates: white ones cut off pajamas now at the dust rag stage; five blue ones left over when I needed just one to put on a suit and the smallest available card held six; seven large black ones cut off my winter coat when I could not match the eighth missing one, and four smaller ones from the sleeves and belt of the same coat. Like a patchwork quilt, the Button Basket held stories of a family's history.

When she was young, Emilie used to love sorting the buttons—by size, by color, by pattern. On many afternoon visits she would ask to play with them, spill them on my bed, and then arrange them in different ways.

"This can be a family," she would say as she put two large green ones next to the five smaller greens. "This one needs a friend; I'll put that tiny blue one next to it."

Sometimes the arrangement did not have a story but rather an interesting pattern, and sometimes she separated by size: "All the little ones go in this corner, the middle sized ones over here, and the big ones across here." "Grandma, these gold ones could be for a princess."

Often, if I saw a special button or set, I would buy it and add it to the basket's contents. A dressmaker friend, learning about Emilie, watched for interesting buttons for me.

When she became ten, Emilie no longer asked to play with the buttons. Because I wanted her to have a memory of those special afternoons we shared, I wrapped the basket for her birthday.

Later I sent her a letter with the story of her present.

"Dear Emilie," I wrote, "I promised to tell you the history of the Button Basket, and as you will see, the basket is part of history itself. It was given to me by the wife of the President of the United States at a party held at Mount Vernon, the home of the first president of our country. The party was one of many events held in connection with the signing of the Panama Canal Treaty in 1978.

"The Canal had been built by the United States in the years from 1904-1914. After completion it was managed by U.S. military stationed in that strip of Panama that we controlled. Although our country paid rent every year for use of the land, Panama now wanted to reclaim it for themselves. They wanted to take over the Canal management and to be without foreign (U.S.) troops on their soil.

"President Carter believed this was right, and he asked negotiators to find a way to gradually transfer control to Panama while insuring that the canal would always remain open to ships of all countries. After many long meetings, an agreement was reached. It was ratified by Panama and by the U.S. Senate (this was not easy).

"To celebrate the accomplishment, representatives of Panama, of Congress, of the U.N., of Caribbean and South American countries, and American Ambassadors to those countries were invited to Washington. Your grandfather was then the U.S. Ambassador to Jamaica, and we flew home for the ceremonies.

"It was on the second day of special events that your basket appeared. For the many women attending the celebration, Mrs. Carter, wife of the President, and Mrs. Vance, wife of the Secretary of State, planned a luncheon journey on the Potomac River. We were invited to board the ship in Washington, sail down the river while we were served lunch and then disembark at Mount Vernon for a tour of George Washington's home and estate.

"The luncheon was impressive for many reasons. First, of course, it was fun to have a lovely meal while sailing down a river. But even more impressive was the detailed planning that went into the event. Seated at each round table, was a mix of diplomatic wives, congressional wives, foreign wives. For the first half of the meal, Mrs. Carter circulated among tables on deck A, and Mrs. Vance, on Deck B. For the second half the two hostesses changed places so that every guest could talk with both of them.

"When we docked at Mount Vernon, uniformed military aides were waiting to escort us up the slope to the mansion. Each woman was greeted by an aide who spoke her own native language, and stayed by her side as long as she wished. I heard French, Spanish, Portuguese, and more. After being shown through the house, we were served afternoon tea and cool drinks on that lovely lawn overlooking the river. As often as I had visited Mount Vernon before, this beautiful sunny afternoon was the first time I found myself thinking how much George Washington must have loved it there. I thought, also, how appropriate it was to be at this home today. This man who did so much to achieve our country's independence, would have approved our voluntarily increasing the independence of Panama by granting them control of their own territory.

"After refreshments, when it was time to leave, the uniformed aides escorted each visitor through the gardens to the postern gate. There, one of a group of waiting ladies handed me a basket with my name on it. "Thank you for coming, Mrs. Irving," she said. "This is a memento of your visit to Mount Vernon." Inside the basket, nested in green florist paper, were packets of herbs and seeds from the Mount Vernon gardens.

"I do not know what I did with the herbs and the seeds from Mount Vernon, but because I really liked the basket, I put it where I would see it every day. That is how it came to sit in my bedroom and hold buttons. I'm sure that practical woman, Martha Washington, would have approved.

"So, dear granddaughter, this is the story of your present. On a special occasion, one I was proud to be part of, the basket was a gift from the wife of the President of the United States to the wife of the U.S. Ambassador to Jamaica, and now it is a gift from your grandmother to you.

"I am very glad I gave it to you. On your tenth birthday you opened all your presents and were appreciative, as you always are. Your last package was the tissue-wrapped basket. As you pulled away the paper, you smiled at me your largest smile of the day, 'It's the Button Basket!'

"It's yours now, Emilie. Who knows what lies ahead for the Button Basket or for you?

"Love, Grandma."

Flowers I Have Known

I do not have a green thumb. It is not into my care that vacationing friends entrust their houseplants. Still I do have one horticultural achievement. In Jamaica I opened a flower show.

The newspaper picture shows me sitting on the stage at the Jamaica National Flower show. I am wearing my favorite yellow pants suit and white sandals, and am about to pronounce the show officially open. I am smiling.

"You always have your picture in the paper," begrudged the French Ambassador's wife when she saw it. "You are involved in everything. How do you do it?"

To use her own words it was by becoming involved. When we wanted some plants for the garden of the Residence, my husband and I had gone to the local garden shop to select them ourselves. We enjoyed walking between the rows of plants, seeing both familiar and unfamiliar items, the display beds raised to waist level as in garden shops we had known at home. We enjoyed talking with the shop's owner. On our third visit, she told us she was a member of Jamaica's Horticultural Society, and asked if we would be willing to open the spring flower show. We were delighted to accept. My smile in the photograph was genuine.

In Jamaica, even my un-green thumb could grow things. To my constant amazement, I could cut a slip from a rose bush, place it in the ground, water it, and know it would root and bloom. In December and January the entire front of our guesthouse was covered with a bank of poinsettias, seven feet tall. Orchids hung from a tree in the back garden. Bananas grew on a tree near staff quarters. Mangoes grew on the palm tree near the front door. Although to see that tree was to bring back memories of a Peace Corps Director, briefly our houseguest. The day of a large party we were hosting for her, she spotted a ripe mango high in the palm. With complete lack of concern for the press of activities required of a household staff the day of a large function, she asked one of them to climb the tree and pick the mango for her. My husband and I were more than a little irked when we heard of this. This same woman on arrival from Washington had asked me if I would have my staff wash and iron her best clothes; she had been too busy before she left home to see to it. I said that she should know I washed my own best things myself, by hand. We did not wash her dresses.

This woman irritated everyone. When the Embassy officers learned her stay could be shortened a day if it were not for the cost of a plane ticket from Kingston to Montego Bay airport, they all voted to pitch in to buy the ticket. At that meeting, my husband injected, "I think you should save a share to let Mrs. Irving contribute. She has suffered more than the rest of us."

But I digress from my gardening conversation.

Jamaica was our only tropical posting and my interest in the variety of flowers brought many friends there. The wife of the Minister of Social Services came to help me in my garden one day. She pointed out the poisonous plants growing there, plants any Jamaican would recognize. "If you ever get this sap on your hands, Dorothy," she warned, "do not touch your face or your eyes. Just wash your hands immediately." We became good friends in the garden. When I left her country she gave me an illustrated book of Jamaica's beautiful flowers.

In New Zealand, too, we found poisonous plants in our garden. I asked the gardener to pull them up. "It's only poisonous if you break the stem and get any sap in your mouth," he told me. But with our four-year-old daughter and her friends playing in the yard, I saw no need to keep the plants. The gardener took care of our whole neighborhood, giving one day a week to each of five families on our street. I could not blame my neighbors for assigning Monday to the newcomer, temporary resident, but I was secretly amused that our house was the one always shortchanged by New Zealand's many Monday holidays.

In New Zealand it was not orchids or roses, but camellias that filled the garden. White, pink, pink and white, deep rose, they blossomed on bushes taller than I. When I was in high school, a single camellia was a beautiful corsage. Now I kept the fragrant flowers in every room of our home.

At our first post, Vienna, we found flowers, fruits, and vegetables growing in the Himmelstrasse garden. In the summer an Austrian friend helped me make delicious jams from our apricot trees and raspberry bushes. I have never been able to duplicate the wonderful results I produced under her guidance.

In Iceland, our most northern post, gardening was different. My first fall there, I planted jonquil bulbs. In July the leaves were about four inches tall. In Iceland I did not see the lush and rich blooms of the tropics nor even the azaleas and rhododendrons I knew at home. I learned to love the small flowers, the many plants that grew and bloomed among the lava. These tiny flowers—here not outshone by taller more brilliant blooms—were treasures to find. Many years after leaving Iceland, in the first small flowers of spring I feel a memory of that awareness learned in the north.

In Iceland, we came to treasure flowers in small numbers. On my hall table for parties, next to the guest book I always stood two roses in bud vases. On our long dining room table, I arranged red and white carnations in three silver Revere bowls, often pointing out that Paul Revere was a silversmith from the early days of New England. In Iceland, flowers were usually given in odd numbers. If I took flowers to a friend it might be three or five. The day I went with the Prime Minister's wife to visit her daughter in the hospital, I carried five roses. The girl's mother carried seven. In that northern country, the second best Christmas present was a plant. Books were always first, but after them came hyacinths, tulips, jonquils in pots. Each Christmas, one poetic gentleman brought me a bowl of Icelandic moss he had gathered and shaped. He had filled it with the tiniest of blossoms.

Now that I am home, I am intrigued by the role flowers played in the memories of this woman without a green thumb. Each cut rose I manage to keep alive for four days reminds me of the roses I so casually transplanted in my Jamaican garden. Each whiff of a camellia takes me back to New Zealand, and each hyacinth of Easter returns me to Christmas in Iceland where we received so many of them.

The Woman at Red Hills

Although I saw her only once, her picture stays clear in my mind. The day we met she was standing by an outdoor stove in Jamaica's ninety-five degree heat, stirring a large iron pot. The Red Hills Basic School, a nursery school I had come to visit, was across the yard from where she stood.

During our tour in Jamaica, I had seen many schools in many parts of the country. This was my first visit to Red Hills, a community on the low slopes of the mountains rising behind the capital seaport of Kingston. A Jamaican friend had invited me to go with her and we had a pleasant day. The three teachers showed us around and we talked together of our ideas about early childhood education. The four- and five-year-old children (about thirty of them) were welcoming, friendly, and interested, attractive as are all children of that age. But it is the woman stirring the pot whom I remember.

The "kitchen" area where she stood was a small roofed patio attached to the side of a larger building. The roof, supported by the building on one side and by two poles on its outer edge, kept off Jamaica's occasional torrents and its more frequent tropical sun. Nothing protected the sides.

The stove was a cubical brick structure about three feet high and equally wide. Its center was deep enough to hold small pieces of wood or coke for the fire. More wood was piled waiting on the stone floor nearby. At the time of our meeting that morning, the fire was burning slowly, giving off enough heat to keep the large iron pot simmering. I could smell the bubbling soup inside it, the lunch for the children at the school. The woman was stirring it with a long handled spoon.

I asked my friend if the school employed a cook, not usual in such small schools. "No," was the answer, "she just comes on her own to help."

The woman stood next to the stove barefoot on the stone floor. She was probably near sixty with hair likely lighter than it once had been. As she stirred, her back was straight, her legs firmly placed, her feet a little apart for balance. She wore a short-sleeved cotton print dress with blue and green flowers. I cannot tell you the color of her skin. A gift of living in Jamaica was that after several months there, skin color no longer registered. What I do remember about the woman is her face and her words. Her face had an expression that combined purpose, contentment, caring, and service. "I don't know enough to know how to teach," she told me. "But I want to do something for the children, and so I come every day to help with their meal. Children need all of us. This is all I know how to do, and so I do it." When it was time for me to leave, she turned back to her stove, and it is there I picture her.

I remember her often. I remember her always if I meet pomposity, if I meet someone who says, "There's nothing I know how to do," or someone who doesn't care. I think of her standing there daily by the hot stove to do what she can to help children.

When I remember the woman from Red Hills, I think also of a woman from a land far distant from Jamaica. In a small village of New Zealand at a family cemetery, I read the message on her gravestone. It said simply, "She did the best she could."

Teacher Abroad

On a warm sunny afternoon, on a hilltop in northern Jamaica, I "opened" a school. The night before the opening I had stayed in the village below at the home of a Jamaican friend. On Sunday she drove me up the long dirt road to the one-room cinder block building, which would be the first school for the youngest children in this rural area. Awaiting us were about sixty people, the parents and friends who had paid for the material and done much of the building themselves. There were no other buildings or houses in sight. My friend parked next to the only other car, a Jamaican Police vehicle.

When all were gathered, we moved into the building for the ceremony. Inside was one large room about twenty by thirty feet. It was furnished with unmatched chairs, benches, and tables. In the right front corner stood a wood stove for the mountain's cool wet mornings.

In Jamaica there is a ritual for a school opening. After prayers and speeches (Jamaican speeches do not customarily use one word if six will do), the "opening" begins. As honored guest, I was asked to open the front door, a process of walking to the door, opening it, declaring, "I now pronounce this door open," and putting a small donation in a basket nearby. After me, others "opened" the windows, the books, the chairs, the tables. Anything that could be opened was an excuse for a speech and a reason to give a little money. There was much clapping and laughter as people sought ever more things to open.

When we could find nothing still unopened, the event concluded with a prayer for the children who would come tomorrow, and we moved outside for refreshments and conversation. At that point I had to speak to the security guard who had spent the entire afternoon sitting next to the wood stove, his eyes never leaving my face. Inside I had ignored him and hoped the others had too, but when he stepped between me and the parents outside, I asked him to stand back. "No one here will harm me," I assured him. What was the point of my being there if I was going to be "protected" from the people I had come to meet?

My involvement in schools started soon after our arrival. The Embassy press release on my husband and myself (the Embassy Officer included mine only at my husband's insistence) described my experience in education and social work, giving me credentials right away.

As soon as the newspaper articles appeared, the University of the West Indies invited me to become part of their demonstration preschool. A select private school asked me to be on their staff, "Just come when you can."

It was not hard to turn down the private school. I have always preferred working in public schools, and I felt that that particular school wanted not my teaching experience but the prestige of having a connection to the "American Ambassador's wife." I would have enjoyed working at the University. The research and the work with children would have been fun, and I knew I would like the sense of belonging to a staff, of being greeted as a co-worker when I came in. It could be easier than approaching new school after new school. I chose the wider route for two reasons. American representation had been very poor in Kingston; American families had stayed close to the Embassy, socializing only with each other or within the diplomatic corps. I felt it was important to show that many Americans get involved in their communities, and important, too, to meet Jamaicans beyond those in the highest circles of government.

So I reached out.

First, I asked the Minister of Education if it would be all right if I visited schools in his country. He assured me that such interest would be welcome. "If you need any help in planning visits, call on my office."

"When I heard nothing," he said later, "I assumed Dorothy's request had been simply the courteous interest of a newcomer or that she found Embassy responsibilities taking all her time. Then suddenly she was everywhere, at schools all over Jamaica, meeting each month with the Early Childhood supervisors at their request, helping to lead training workshops and even bringing back plans and programs from the United States for our new Early Childhood Resource Center. Although many contributed money for the Center, and we thank them, it was Dorothy's personal involvement that people remember."

It was my personal involvement that I remember, too.

Pictures crowd into my head when I think of the schools I came to know. I recall the evening I gave out prizes to graduates from a school-leavers program, a place for girls who had dropped out of school, then returned and completed their courses. The Director thanked me for doing them the honor of taking part in the ceremony; I said it was the girls who brought honor to the event, they, their teachers, and the proud parents who had stood behind them. I, who had gone through school without interruption, saluted the courage and determination of these new graduates.

And I remember the morning I walked into a country pre-school, a school with few toys, no running water, and a room about ten by twelve. Thirty children tightly crowded on wooden benches sat facing the one window. They were singing happily about how much they had to be thankful for. I wonder if their loving teacher knows I carry that picture in my heart. And the even smaller school: five benches on the porch of a Kingston home, with children squeezed five to a bench as they sang and recited together. It was at this school I first heard the common use of "Teacher" for any friendly adult at the school. In Washington, kindergartners, especially when hurt or worried, would often call a loved teacher "Mom," but "Teacher, Teacher," as an attention getter was new to me.

In all of these schools I read stories, played word games, led my favorite nursery school songs. "Fly away Little Birdie" was enjoyed as much in Jamaica as it had been in Maryland. A newspaper photo of me at the Rastafarian pre-school shows me and the children all with our arms outstretched, obviously being birds in the middle of the "Fly Away" song.

I spent many hours at the Rastafarian school up in the hills of Kingston. Jamaican friends worried about my safety there, but I had made my first visit to the school with a Jamaican teacher. After that, the school knew why I was coming, and the clusters of teenagers with knives in their belts at the door did not worry me. Soon they smiled and returned my greetings. A surprise at the Rastafarian school one morning was the unscheduled visit of their supervisor. I was seated on a small chair in a circle of children. We were telling a story together, and I was unaware of the supervisor's arrival. She often said later, how surprised she was to walk in and see the wife of the American Ambassador on that small chair working with those children. She said it made her rethink the lessons she had been taught on her Castro-sponsored training session in Cuba. She and I still correspond.

Whenever, with the demands of Embassy life, I felt tired or pressed for time, I realized the only part of my schedule I could drop would be my work with the schools. This was something I would not do. Instead I promised myself to keep the next free day (perhaps two weeks hence) unscheduled, and rest then. My work in schools was important to me as part of who I was, not only an Ambassador's wife, but also a teacher. I knew, too, that my work enhanced the effectiveness of the Embassy. The American business community thanked me publicly for, "improving the climate in which we conduct business." And at a meeting one day the Prime Minister told my husband, "Please tell Dorothy that because of her I am moving the improvement of Early Childhood Education from my third five year plan to my first."

When we left Jamaica, the Prime Minister showed his awareness and appreciation of my efforts in his country. At the farewell luncheon he gave us, half the guests were from the Ministry of Foreign Affairs in honor of my husband, and—a great courtesy to me—the other half were from the Ministry of Education. At the Foreign Minister's parting lunch, the guests were all from the fields of education and social work. "This lunch is really for Dorothy," he told my husband, "though protocol demands I say it is for the Ambassador." The Minister of Security, the man responsible for safety of diplomats in his country, wrote a farewell note to my husband that read, "We are sorry to see you go, but must you take Dorothy with you? She is irreplaceable." This was the man who had once complained that I was too active, that my trips used up too much of his staff's time. "At least," he said when he took us out for a farewell dinner, " I won't have to be sending my men chasing you all over the country now."

As time came to leave Jamaica, I realized how fortunate had been my choice to work in many different schools. Because of those schools my personal links spread wide across that island country. I had traveled from Appleton, to Savannah la Mar, to St. Elisabeth's, to Kingston. At our farewell reception two days before we left, I felt the warmth that the schools and I had shared. Several teachers brought me posters made by their children. One was signed by each child, the names in varied sizes and colors. Another had bright pictures of Jamaica's flowers. A third had hand prints outlined by four year olds, a name carefully lettered inside each hand. One poster offered the traditional Jamaican farewell, the wish used by country and city people alike: in large rainbow colored letters, the children had spelled out, "Walk Good."

I treasured these warm farewells, but the tribute that brought tears to my eyes came many months later back in New York City. An American businessman with whom we were having dinner seemed to know a great deal of what I had done in Jamaica. This was the first time I had met him, and I expressed surprise that he knew so much about my activities. Over our dessert of fresh raspberries (in January!), he looked at me, "Don't you know what they say about you there? In Jamaica they call you America's answer to Castro. They say Castro came to Jamaica and built large schools on the highways where everyone could see them, but Dorothy Irving came to Jamaica, went to schools all over the country, and helped our children learn."

WE COME HOME

Life After the Foreign Service

Most Recent Occupation

I never put it in my written resumé. A personnel officer reading it would smile silently, "We really don't need anyone to pour tea," and the application would go into the out-box labeled, "Turn down politely." If the title slipped out in a job interview, the eyes of the prospective employer would glaze as he thought, "How quickly can I end this interview and say no to this person?"

So I tried not to say I'd been an Ambassador's wife. It closed too many doors. In all fairness, I could understand. On hearing the phrase, does one think of a woman scrubbing fingerprints off Embassy walls (because the floor cleaners said it wasn't their job, and the window cleaners did only windows, and the President of her country was due the next day)? Or of someone (with her daughter's help) painting the Residence laundry room a cheery bright yellow? To even wonder if such painting might be needed, you would have to know that the State Department decorates only the public rooms, not the basement work areas. Would you readily assume the Ambassador's wife drew up the architectural plans for a needed new kitchen—after the Washington architects sent out a drawing that suggested they had never prepared or served a meal—and that her plans were accepted and built; that she cared for staff members' sick children, carried homemade chicken soup to a bedridden first tour officer (who later grew up to be an Ambassador)?

Behind the smiling face in the receiving line does one picture the organization that went into planning a four-day schedule for official house guests, with meetings, meals, cars, contacts arranged and coordinated; with detailed lists left each day for the household staff, because the organizer-hostess would be busy with those house guests?

When we hear that officials of disparate political views are brought together in a home, do we think of the weeks of building trust that made this possible? Do we think of the effort and perseverance in learning another country's language and customs, in fitting a family happily into a new community every few years? or of the experience of group leadership and public speaking?

Does the personnel officer assume that this woman across from him read and, when necessary, translated every daily paper to sense local feeling towards America? Can he know that this particular wife was so involved in furthering U.S. interests abroad that the State Department gave her one of the first full security clearances given to a wife, thus enabling her to have available any information she needed?

When the interviewer pictures a lady pouring tea, does he realize that before filling the cup, the Ambassador's wife first counted it—along with every other cup in the Residence; also every spoon, fork, knife, goblet, dish, chair, table, bed, tablecloth, sheet, towel; that she signed for each item on arrival at post, and then counted and accounted for each of them on departure? No, I'm afraid the mind stays with the tea party or the receiving line.

The Department of State once asked selected Ambassadors' wives to keep track for two weeks of how much time we spent directly on Embassy business. I think we all kept our records meticulously. The responses showed more hours that had been expected. My first week was sixty-eight hours actual time; my second was seventy-one.

Not too many of them had been spent pouring tea!

Happy Fourth Of July
(First Year At Home)

This Fourth of July I shall do nothing, nothing, and nothing. Well, not entirely nothing. I shall put out the flag; I shall be glad that I am an American, that I believe in the ideals of this country. I shall be glad that, although we sometimes fail, we intend to value every person equally: we intend that every person shall have the right to life, liberty, and the pursuit of happiness. I shall be glad that at times we feel like one united nation. And I shall think of how I can help to make this feeling a constant reality and not just a dream.

The "nothing" I shall do is: no parties, no barbecues, no scheduled feasts, not even a gathering of friends. After being part of a U.S. Embassy for many years, I have a slightly different view of celebrating the Fourth.

Every Embassy abroad proudly celebrates its country's national day. Every July 14, the French observe Bastille Day; on June Fifth the Danish celebrate; on June seventeenth, the Icelanders; and we, on the Fourth of July. At such national day celebrations, community leaders and members of the host government are invited, as are ambassadors of other countries. Some representatives of the celebrating country may also be included. In the early part of the twentieth century, when Americans traveled less than they do today, the Fourth of July was open house at the Ambassador's residence for any American in the country on that holiday. Today with increasing numbers of travelers, this is no longer possible. The Ambassador's reception is by invitation, not by nationality. Even so, the guest list can number in the hundreds.

In the 1950s when my husband and I started in the Foreign Service, embassies were like small kingdoms with the Ambassador the king (and his wife, the queen). Everyone on the staff was required to help with Fourth of July preparations. In New Zealand in 1964, as the wife of a mid-level officer, I was assigned two hundred small cakes and three hundred small sandwiches. Wherever we live, we let our children stay out of school on the Fourth, but that New Zealand day, I had little time to celebrate with them. If they wanted to talk with me, the three of them came to the kitchen to watch or to help fix those five hundred small items. They rode with me to deliver my contribution to the Ambassador's residence. Our biggest family celebration was a red, white, and blue cake at home before I had to dress for the official reception. Senior and mid-level officers were expected to attend, to circulate at the party and "help" with the guests. Families of lower level officers also helped prepare the food, but were not invited to the reception. As my husband and I left for the New Zealand party, we drove our children to a friend's house for the evening.

In 1972 when my husband first became an ambassador, times had changed; rights of royalty no longer went with the job. If we wanted to serve x-hundred small sandwiches, the making of them or the hiring of someone to do it was our responsibility. I'm sure I could not have asked of others, the kind of service once asked of me, even if such personal demands had not—correctly—been banished from an embassy representing a democratic country. I planned the menu and found people to help our household staff prepare it. We started cooking weeks ahead and froze as much as possible; U.S. Government funds did not assume outside catering expenses. As July Fourth approached, I arranged for extra serving people, for extra trays and glasses, for all the preparations necessary for a party with many guests.

Together, my husband and I planned the guest list, ordered the invitations, and decided where we would hold the reception. Ambassadors, whose homes, like ours in Reykjavík, were small, often planned their national day celebrations for a hotel or a large hall. Others did what we chose to do, held the party at home, but moved out most of the furniture. The living room was not very homelike when emptied of couches, tables and chairs, but we wanted our guests to come to the place that was our home and the official home of the United States in their country. We wanted them to be able to say they had been to the American Embassy not to the Saga or the International Hotel. When the numbers were too large to fit at one time, we staggered the reception over several hours. Guests were invited to come from two to four, three to five, or four to six. We sorted names for each time period.

Each of our four years in Iceland we planned such staggered receptions. Three were very happy events: one we remember with less joy. On the third of July our third year, we were told a group of young American scientists were in Reykjavík and would like to be included in the reception. We invited them for the latest period of time when they would be with Icelanders from the university and scientific community, people they might enjoy talking with. We told them that it was a "suit and tie" reception; we didn't want them to expect a barbecue. So we were a little surprised when all six arrived wearing old jeans, some torn, painter's caps worn both forwards and backwards. (They resisted a request to remove them.) Amid the professional circle of dark suits and party dresses our American scientists stood out. In addition they acted as if it was the first time they had ever seen free drinks. I remember the sigh that escaped the young Danish girl who was helping us that year. In Denmark they feel almost as strongly about the Fourth as we do, and she had been looking forward to her first, "American Fourth," as she put it. After finding his coat for the last departing scientist, and fending off several aggressive invitations to join their group for the evening, she came into the living room and said in exhaustion, "So, THAT'S the Fourth of July!"

"Not always," I answered. "Not always."

In warm countries receptions could be held out-of-doors. The last Fourth of July we hosted was in our garden in Jamaica. There was plenty of space for the five hundred who came. At most national day receptions one saw the same people: representatives of government, of other embassies, community leaders. The many Jamaican cabinet members who attended our Kingston party told us they liked to come to the Irvings. "We meet a wide cross section of our countrymen at your house," said one, adding with a smile, "That's always a good thing for elected officials." In addition to the usual guests, we included a variety of friends: Miss Lou, the beloved leader of children's' television—shows we loved too—came; so did leaders of the National Dance group, and of the Jamaican Folk Singers; also, business people, teachers I had met in my school travels, social workers, women leaders I had come to know. The most dramatic arrival our last year was a group of twelve Rastafarians from a school where I had taught. Led by their "Brother Sam," colorfully dressed and with his walking stick cane, they walked up our long driveway in single file procession. The three children among them were shining-eyed during the whole reception. One of my favorite photographs of the day is of my husband stooping to talk to the youngest child at eye level, both of them smiling broadly.

We had many happy July Fourths abroad, and we felt proud to be our country's official representatives on that day. In the midst of each reception, we forgot the many days of preparation that had preceded it and did not think of the day of recovery, which would follow. The American flag that flew in our yard was usually raised by a member of the staff. On the Fourth of July, I raised and lowered it myself.

But now that we are retired, have returned home, and are plain American citizens, we prefer to celebrate by ourselves. We hope you have a very joyous holiday and share it with as many people as will make you happy. We hope you will understand if, this year, we do not invite you over to celebrate with us.

These Shoes Walked At Ephesus

I call them my Ephesus shoes. They may look like ordinary loafers to you—needing a polish now and resoling soon—but I cannot polish or resole them. These shoes walked at Ephesus. They walked upon roads the Romans and the Ephesians walked. They stepped where the physician, Galen, stepped. They stood where the disciple, Paul, stood. These shoes walked at Ephesus.

For much of my life I had wanted to go to Turkey. I don't know why. After college I sent for papers to teach at the American School in Izmir or at Roberts College in Istanbul. The urge was very strong. When my husband and I went into the U.S. Foreign Service, we were sent to Austria and Jamaica, to Iceland and New Zealand, but never to Turkey.

After our retirement the opportunity finally came. My husband was called back by the State Department to lead a team in negotiations regarding U.S. properties in Cyprus and Turkey, and I was asked to examine the schools used by U.S. dependents in those countries. Turkey, at last! Of all the special assignments we might have been given, this was the most wonderful possible. Our itinerary read Athens, Nicosia, Istanbul, Izmir, Ankara.

The first stop was Athens, and the not-yet-Ephesus loafers happily explored the Acropolis. My courses in Art History came alive. Seeing in stone what I had studied in slides was like meeting old friends. The following day these shoes walked the paths of Delphi, high in the Greek mountains. In the stunning and awesome beauty of its location, the Greeks had chosen well this home for their oracle. Here it was easy to feel a melding of nature, god, and man.

A friend visiting Iceland had told me he felt this awe also at Thingvellir, the geographically dramatic home of Iceland's first outdoor parliament. He said the two places on earth where he was most aware of the impact of nature on man's spirit were the grandeur of that Icelandic gorge, and the heights of Mount Delphi.

From Greece we flew to Cyprus, that cross lanes of history in the eastern Mediterranean, a country inhabited without interruption since prehistoric times. Seafarers, settlers, conquerors, traders, left their mark on the land, offering us today layers of civilization and history. My loafers walked through the streets of old Nicosia, where always-friendly shopkeepers redirected me each time I was lost. We walked at the Greek ruins and the Roman theater of Salamis, and—going even further back in time—at the prehistoric city of Enkomi (from 1800 B.C.). By 1500 B.C., Enkomi was a center of the copper trade and the largest city in Cyprus. Its excavated streets still lay at perfect right angles; its square houses outlined by building stones found on the site, stones now laid one to two feet high. From afar it looked a little like a large stone waffle spread on the ground. At this unguarded, open city, my loafers stepped very lightly. We were there to visit, not to disturb.

Then, at last, it was on to Turkey. Fred spent several days negotiating about government properties there. For me, after two days at the schools, I was on my own and free to explore. I walked the bazaars and the side streets of Istanbul. Stopping one morning at a fruit stand for oranges, I heard the proprietor call the oranges, "Portugals."

"That's a strange name for them," I commented.

"It's no more strange than calling a certain bird a Turkey," he replied. I was silent!

A few days later I walked in Ankara, in the shops and streets of the old city. And then, as a special birthday-Christmas-everything present to myself, I went for a day to the Hittite sites in Eastern Turkey, those hilltop remains of a once great kingdom: Bogazkoy, Yazihkaya. Carvings from 1400 B.C. were still clear, a profiled line of worshipers on the rock wall of an outdoor temple, and two lions on the eight foot gates which had been the entry to the large city. My loafers walked in the temple, climbed over stones of the once-city, and walked through the opening of that narrow lion gate. The shoes were the underpinning that held me erect as I stopped between the gateposts, standing proudly in the February wind looking across a field of nothing to picture what once had been.

We Come Home

With all these wonders under their soles, the loafers had already had an exciting trip before they reached Ephesus, but it is because of Ephesus that I save them. The city had been so carefully excavated that in its partial restoration, I could easily picture the Ephesians going about their daily lives. The city felt alive as if its people had left yesterday, a feeling enhanced, I am sure, by the presence of many visitors the day we went. Much remains of what once was there. As I walked the marble road, I could feel the beat of Roman legions marching down to the bay and sea beyond. I could imagine sandaled Ephesians stopping to pay homage at the many small temples and statues that lined the main street. I could picture the physician, Galen, strolling as he thought about medicine and medical knowledge. I sat in the Roman amphitheater and could hear the apostle Paul trying to preach to the Ephesians. Beyond his imaginary figure I could see the two-story facade of the large Çelsus Library. Four pairs of columns supported each floor, and broad steps led up to its three entrances. At one time manuscripts in the form of scrolls or volumes had been stored inside, available for use in a large reading room—perhaps not so different from use of our libraries of today. As we walked back up the main street, I saw a small stone path leading off to the left. Its marker read St. Paul's Way. I could not just walk past it. Quietly, I went by myself about thirty yards up the way until the stones became grass and the wall of the adjoining building ended. I don't know where the path once led, but the apostle Paul had once walked it. I turned back and rejoined the group.

Before the trip was over, my loafers went on to other explorations—also exciting, also memorable. But nothing could compare to the experience of Ephesus. These shoes walked at Ephesus. I cannot refurbish them, nor throw them out, nor give them away. My Ephesus shoes are the lower left pair on my closet shoe rack. I see them every day

Retirement

A Foreign Service friend once said that everything she learned in her years at home in the States went into her Foreign Service life. After we retired, I learned the reverse is also true. All your Foreign Service experience comes home with you.

Think of the lessons we learned during those traveling years. First, that the future is unpredictable. Often as a young woman in Washington, I would plant bulbs in the fall and wonder if I would be there in the spring to see them bloom. Each October as I enjoyed autumn's colors I wondered, "Will I see them again next year?" I used to tell our children that no one really knows what lies ahead; in the Foreign Service we know we don't know. Another April of springtime blooms, another fall of colored leaves, another year at our local school, were only possibilities.

Each time we chose what to pack for an overseas tour, we relearned what was important to us. When our possessions were lost or broken in transit, we learned how much or how little they meant to us. If we returned from a tour with a box never unpacked during our stay, we re-examined the worth of its contents. When we said goodbye to friends and neighbors, we learned how central our family unit was in our lives.

We had a lot of practice in saying goodbye. The partings from people we cared about were often final farewells and we knew it at the time. Practice did not make goodbyes any easier, just more familiar. How true this is in retirement. Frequency of final farewells does not make them easier.

Perhaps our motives in joining the Foreign Service contributed to our ease in retirement. We had not joined the service for its prestige or to see the world. In the idealism of the 1940s we joined to serve our country. It was not the travel but the contributions we could make that drew us. Now that we are home, overseas travel holds little allure. We are eager to see as much of our own country as we can. We are happy to revisit a favorite post, but we have had much exploring of new posts and new customs. Mostly we are satisfied to stay put. My husband's statement is that he wants only contiguous land travel. He wants to be able to walk home if he wishes. Is this because we served in three island countries (New Zealand, Jamaica, Iceland), and in one city (occupied Vienna), a landlocked capital surrounded by territory we could not enter?

I don't know what use our children have made of one special Foreign Service skill—how to behave in an airport. With schedules and travel being carefully arranged, we had a rule that once we were in the airport there was to be no wandering apart from the family. Our three children would carry in their share of luggage, and then go sit on the nearest airport bench or seats, never stirring until we were called to board the plane. Once, when they were young adults, and our family was flying from D.C. to Boston, I looked over at them in Washington's National Airport. There they sat as properly at eighteen, twenty-two, twenty-four as they had at four, eight and ten. Will they still do it at fifty, fifty-four, fifty-six?

Even my experience in learning other languages offered a skill, practical in retirement. Sometimes, when speaking Icelandic or German, I wanted to use a word I didn't know or couldn't remember. As soon as I saw the verbal gap looming ahead of me, I would modify my sentence so the word wasn't needed. Yesterday, when a word escaped me, I used the same approach, revising my sentence midstream to go around the absent word. It was never missed.

Shortly after our final return to America, I chaired the fortieth reunion of my college class. As I had helped my husband on so many projects, he now helped me on this. A classmate commented. "You two work so well together. Even without telling each other what needs doing, whoever sees it first, steps in and does it." Some of these traits we had developed in our diplomatic years. Working together for a common goal, we came to recognize and respect each other's achievements and abilities. While becoming acquainted with each new community, we were each other's mutual support system.

And finally, we work together in planning what happens when we die. We discussed it one morning at breakfast.

Fred spoke first. "As an ex POW, with a Purple Heart, and with my government positions, I am entitled to be buried in Arlington National Cemetery. I would like us to be buried there if you agree."

"You are entitled to be buried there by your record of service. I am entitled only as your wife. I would be both proud and humble to be buried there, because, although I was not in a war, I did serve my country both overseas and at home. I would come to Arlington as a citizen who served to the best of her ability."

He looked at me. "It is because of you that I want us to do this. I have never felt the U.S. Government or the State Department gave you the credit you deserved for all you did. I would like to know you will be buried in the nation's highest cemetery."

Stairs Of My Life

Stairs have led up and down throughout the years of my life. Joy or worry could wait in either direction.

On the first stairs I remember, worry predominated. Childhood surgeries meant having a mask put over my mouth, inhaling gas, then ether until I was asleep. Each time this happened I felt myself going down, down, endless cement stairs with a clanging sound that still unnerves me if I hear it. My safety in the trip was my grasping of my parents' hands. One stood on either side of me, both promising they would not let the surgeon cut until I showed I was asleep by letting go of their fingers.

The next cement stairs important to me led upwards to joy, fifteen broad steps into Providence Classical High School. How eager I was to start the new experience and how much I came to love all the years of it. That first day as I walked up the girls' stairway on the right, I had no inkling that climbing the stairs on the left was a fourteen year old boy who would one day become my husband. Four years later, at college, stairs again led up to learning, "Did she have to get a room on the fourth floor?" asked my weary father after his fifth trip up helping me move in. "Sh-h," whispered my mother. "She has a lovely view of the campus from up here."

Those dormitory climbs prepared me well for the housing my Classical High husband and I found when we were first married. In Boston, during graduate school, we had only three flights to climb, but the high ceilings in that old New England boarding house made those three flights long ones. On our move to wartime Washington, the converted room we finally found was a fourth floor walkup. Each morning we thought very carefully of our needs for the day before we went down to the car and to work. When I felt sorry for myself carrying groceries up so many steps, I remembered the tenants we replaced. Their baby was born just two weeks after we had passed each other on the stairs.

With our first house we gladly reduced to one flight of stairs. I smile now to think how much a part of family life that flight became. I remember going up several times an evening to be assured a new healthy baby was still breathing; going up hourly to feel the forehead of a feverish toddler; coming down on Christmas mornings, the impatient children waiting until their slow parents were ready, then marching down, youngest first, to see if Santa had come.

When Susan was little in that first house, going down stairs was a challenge for all of us. We had to be careful not to step on her invisible rabbits and turtles. One at a time, she would carry them down, her two hands cradling each small creature. We were never sure on which step they might be resting, and if she was present we proceeded very cautiously. Once her father stepped on one—learning his mistake only when Susan burst into loud tears. Attempting, as mothers will, to establish the difference between imagination and reality, I once said to her, "Even though we know your rabbit is make believe, it's fun to pretend he's there and he's gray, isn't it?" "Oh," she replied, "The rabbit is only pretend. We know that." "But my turtles are green."

Some years later, Barbara was told to, "just go sit on the stairs for a few minutes," a punishment for some minor infraction. As I went about my household tasks, I heard her singing softly. I was intrigued by her choice of song: "My heart is as free as wind o'er the ocean. My lips may be still, but I think what I will." A Sunday School hymn—it was hard for a mother to object to that; but I think her choice shortened the punishment by at least a few minutes. How could I keep from laughing as I walked by, or from wondering if the choice of hymn was an act of defiance or of courage. Recently I asked her which it had been. She answered (we love each other), "It takes courage to be defiant."

Rick, too, must have memories of those stairs. In reply to an evening teenage question, "When must I be home?" we had answered, "Well, whenever you think. Certainly by two." To us it was obviously a joke; to Rick it was obviously permission. He was no little surprised to return on the dot of two and find his parents sitting on the top stair with less than happy faces.

We Come Home

For a Foreign Service family it is hard not to associate stairs with airports: waiting at the foot of a plane's exit to greet an arriving VIP—a windy occupation in Iceland, a warm one in Jamaica; descending a plane's steps on arrival at a new post, looking down at those assembled to welcome us, and knowing the same question hangs in all our minds: "What will these people be like?" or climbing the steps to a plane on a last departure from a country, pausing at the door to wave goodbye, realizing we would see some of those friends again, but others, never.

Our last departure was from Jamaica, and now we are home to stay.

Recently the steps of our home led down to joy. Fred and I have always chosen to celebrate our wedding anniversary alone—on the assumption that it was a matter that mostly concerned us. On our fiftieth our three children said they wanted to do something special: what would we like? The answer was easy: to have all three families here at the same time, to have a meal together, and to do none of the work ourselves.

Their response was wonderful. From three different cities they planned the day. Tasks were distributed by abilities. The one who makes a dream out of vegetables did the vegetables; the pie maker brought pies; the salad maker, the salad; the one near a garden shop brought a carload of flowers; the artistic one arrived with a carload of balloons; the most distant city dweller brought the champagne. Grandchildren cut up the fruit cup and were everywhere.

About thirty minutes before lunch, Fred and I went up to change and were told to, "Wait until we call you." When permitted to appear, we came down to a fairyland. In our home, the stairs turn midway at a right angle. As we descended, the view from the upper half was closed off completely by a mass of gold and white balloons. We turned at the landing to see white and gold everywhere. The house was beautiful. But the scene we shall never forget was there in the front hall below us: standing in a semicircle were the twelve people we most love—six adults and six children. They smiled and clapped as together we descended those last five stairs.

Acknowledgments

The support of many people made my book possible. I thank them all:
Bobbie and Norman Selverstone for their friendship and support on several fronts, Edward Wolpow and his family for responding enthusiastically to everything I sent them, Cambridge Center writing teacher, Brina Cohen, who was the first to say, "You have a book," the members of her class, who heard most of the stories, and were quick to praise and to correct. I thank them for listening, especially Rick Stafford, Margaret Gooch, Mordena Babich, Jeff Dougherty, Celia Judge. Similarly, members of my "Thursday" writing group: Karen Davis, Tel Sandman, Janet Polansky. Your ears were discerning, and you often gave me the push I needed. And I thank Keith Asarkof, Mary Murray, and all the friends who received copies of chapters and urged me to put them in a book. I thank editor, Diane Nottle, and poet, Ann Carhardt, for reading the entire manuscript, Sue Riter for warm encouragement and valued editing advice. Any errors are mine.

Lastly, I thank my husband and my children. Without them there would have been no story to tell, and without their help no book would have been written. They have my appreciation and my love.

About the Author

Dorothy J. Irving, a graduate of Mount Holyoke College and Columbia University, has been active all of her adult life in interracial and intercultural activities in the United States and overseas. Dorothy is a recipient of honors from organizations in these fields and a recipient, also, of the Mount Holyoke Alumnae Association Sesquicentennial Award, given to only 50 out of 25,000 living graduates, in "recognition of her activities in national and international community relations that have made a significant impact." She has been recognized by leaders of countries where she served with her career diplomat husband, Ambassador Frederick Irving, for her role in easing of tensions in many situations between the United States and other countries. The Irvings were in the Foreign Service for twenty-eight years.

In retirement Dorothy continues her interest in international affairs and in children's education. She and her husband live in eastern Massachusetts, where they are frequently visited by friends from the countries in which they served. She has written articles for local newspapers and college publications; some of them appear in this book.

The Partnership

Printed in the United States
92320LV00006B/19/A